The Authentic Performer

The Authentic Performer

Wearing a Mask and the Effect on Health

Jennie Morton

compton
PUBLISHING

This edition first published 2015 © 2015 by Compton Publishing Ltd.

Registered office: Compton Publishing Ltd, 30 St. Giles', Oxford,

OX1 3LE, UK Registered company number: 07831037

Editorial offices: 3 Wrafton Road, Braunton, EX33 2BT, UK

Web: www.comptonpublishing.co.uk

ISBN 978-1-909082-47-2

A catalogue record for this book is available from the British Library.

Cover illustration:

Cover design: David Siddall, http://www.davidsiddall.com

Set in Adobe Caslon Pro 10pt by Stuart Brown

1   2015

Table of Contents

Dedicated to the memory of
Julie Morton
(1943–2000)

Acknowledgments

I am incredibly fortunate to have encountered some amazing people in my life who have both shaped and supported my journey and to list them all would be a book in its own right. A brief, chance meeting where a single sentence can create a ripple of thought which, perhaps even many years later, becomes a tsunami of inspiration is every bit as important to me as the life-long friendships that I am lucky enough to have enjoyed. So what follows is an acknowledgement of those who have been a significant part of my journey to the completion of this book.

First, I would like to thank those who gave their time so generously to contribute their experiences to this text: Ben Dawson, Stefan Dennis, Francesca Filpi, Paul Roberts and Jon Scott. I am so grateful for your enthusiasm and openness and for your trust in placing your words in my hands.

For their unfailing support during the writing of this book, I thank the following: Bill Morton (my Dad and champion) for his excellent proof-reading skills and for his never-ending support for my (somewhat unconventional) life; Joan Melton PhD who brought her ever-vigilant eye and encyclopaedic knowledge to bear on the content and for her continued support and collaboration; Heidi Gregory for providing the incitement to finally put pen to paper and for her boundless support and friendship.

For maintaining my physical and psychological wellbeing over the years and for teaching me so much about the wonders of the human body and beyond, I thank: Lin Bridgeford, Ercilia de Marco, Riitta Lister and David Nassim – true mentors and exceptional human beings.

Finally, I thank those who have helped to shape the person I am today, have shared and continue to provide unfailing support for my journey with their words of encouragement and the occasional well-placed question(!): Lucien Cairaschi, John Chong, Toby Cruse, Francesca Filpi, Liz Filpi, Ian MacDonald, Paul Mellon, Sophie Pemberton, Paul Roberts, Jonathan Watkins and Belinda Williams.

Thanks, too, to all my patients, students and colleagues from whom I learn every day.

Introduction

The writing of this book really constitutes a personal journey for me. It seeks to explore the many questions that have occurred to me both during my career as a performer and subsequently as an Osteopath caring for performers. I have become more and more intrigued by the connections between who we are as individuals and how this is reflected in our biology and therefore our health. Whilst the world of the performing arts is made up of a diverse range of people, I believe there is much common ground in the experiences we share – from the way we have been trained to the issues we face in navigating life in the profession – all of which play their part in shaping our personalities, coping strategies and ultimately our health.

I am not attempting to write a 'How To' manual (although I hope there will be some useful ideas in the text), but rather I hope to explore the questions that have occurred to me over the years and try to 'join the dots' of the many interesting texts and experiences that I have encountered in my life. I have no formal training in philosophy or psychology and do not claim to be an authority on either subject, but I will be exploring both philosophical and psychological questions, purely from a layman's perspective, in order to analyze how the life of a professional performer fits into the context of the modern world in which we live. I will also be examining how the experiences we have had, from infancy to adulthood, are reflected in our biology and how these can manifest themselves in terms of our health. In this task I stand on the shoulders of giants in the shape of the many authors whose texts have both excited and informed me (and to which I will refer many times in the following chapters), as well as the numerous teachers I have had the privilege to meet in my life. By teachers I mean not only those who do this in a professional capacity, but also friends, family, colleagues, strangers in a chance meeting and, of course, my wonderful patients and students from whom I constantly learn.

Being a performer can often present some contradictions: when one is required to constantly play a role, this can sometimes lead one further away from one's true self. However, some performers may be attracted to the world of the arts specifically because of this particular opportunity it affords – it can be a good place to hide. The modern world has also changed the nature of our relationship with art: when art becomes a profession and one relies upon it for one's income, this can prove challenging and attach an anxiety to one's natural expression. This is the antithesis of the true role of art and can represent a dichotomy which may have a negative effect on the health of the performer. This text will be exploring both the biological and societal ramifications of the commercialization of art.

Whilst I write this from the perspective of a performer, these themes are not exclusive to the lives of performing artists. How many people outside this profession find themselves 'playing a role' in their own lives, be it through choosing a career that does not suit them, or being stuck in a relationship where their own needs are suppressed? The title *The Authentic Performer* is about achieving true authenticity as human beings, whatever our walk of life, as I firmly believe the path to authenticity also leads to health.

This book may well raise more questions than it asks. If that is so, then I have achieved my aim, for I firmly believe that our society and culture has reached a point where we have become so goal-oriented and focused on fixed targets of achievement, that we are in danger of losing the wonder of the circular and reciprocal forces which are at the roots of our biology, of art itself, and the very nature of the universe in which we live. In going against these forces, we are in danger of producing a negative effect on our health, both as individuals and as a society. Life itself is an abstract concept but science is predicated upon questioning it: but would we not sometimes do better just to wonder? Would you want to live in a world where everything was known, where nothing was left to be discovered, where there was nothing left to

The connection between authenticity and health

An 'authentic' performance is seen as the Holy Grail of the performing arts and something most artists would aspire to produce, but what is it about authenticity that makes it so aspirational? Most audiences will agree when they have witnessed a truly authentic performance, but what exactly is it to which they are connecting? Is it simply about witnessing an excellent representation of some musical repertoire, or a creative interpretation of choreography, or is there something more fundamentally physiological happening to both the performer and the audience? What is it about particular artists that draws us to seek out their performances time and again? Equally, in my work as an Osteopath specializing in treating performing artists, it has often been my experience that some performers find it difficult to leave their characters behind and return to their authentic selves once they leave the performance arena – they appear always to be playing a role. My observation has been that those who seem to be further removed from their true selves, who remain in performance mode even after the curtain has fallen or the camera has stopped rolling, appear to take longer to heal, or to find a resolution to their symptoms. These are some of the concepts, connections and questions that began a process of enquiry which led to my writing this book. To begin our exploration, we need to delve into the composition of this incredible unit of mind and body which we all possess, see how it has developed over millennia in response to our environment and our socio-cultural experiences, and how it influences and is influenced by the world in which we live. This may seem a rather mammoth task for one book, but I hope to synthesize the wealth of detailed information and research on this subject down to a more conceptual level, creating a bird's eye view from which the reader may choose to launch their own investigative path. I beg the forgiveness of those esteemed authors and researchers whose very detailed work I have attempted to condense, but hope that I have succeeded in retaining the 'authenticity' of the themes I shall be exploring.

So how does authenticity connect to health? Let us first explore what we mean by the word authentic. A glance into any dictionary will throw up descriptions such as 'not false or copied', 'genuine', 'real'. Therefore, authenticity is the quality of being authentic or showing genuineness. An authentic person would then be someone who is truly inhabiting his or her genuine self and not displaying an altered version of his or her self to the world – not 'wearing a mask'. So why would we feel it necessary to hide behind a mask? When we interact with other human beings what we 'see' in the other people is what we would describe as their personality: a collection of qualities which have become the visible aspect of the person. But is this 'personality' really genuine? The word 'persona' actually derives from the Latin word for theatrical mask – 'per' meaning 'by way of' and 'sona' meaning sound or spoken word. Speech and sounds were passed through the mask in order to assume another identity or character. In Jungian psychology, it describes the mechanism by which a person conceals their true thoughts and feelings. So do our personalities provide a means to mask our authentic selves? A year ago I had the great pleasure of meeting the award-winning author and physician Gabor Maté MD at a Performing Arts Medicine conference in Toronto at which we were both speakers. Dr Maté worked for many years as a palliative care physician and is also renowned for his work on addictions. His approach is to explore the personal journeys that led these people to their diseases in order to understand the role that emotions and stress play in the development of ill health. Among the many epiphanies and 'light bulb moments' I experienced during his presentation was his statement that we do not have personalities, we have coping strategies. The visible aspect of ourselves which we display to the world is a culmination of our life experiences and the ways in which we have adapted ourselves to deal with them. Taking this concept further, these experiences have not only shaped our so-called personalities, but they have also shaped us at a biological level and therefore may affect our health and also play a role in predicting the type of illnesses to which we may become vulnerable as individuals.

In his book *When the Body Says No: Exploring the Stress-Disease Connection*, Dr Maté refers to an emerging field of medicine called Psychoneuroimmunoendocrinology[2,p.6] or the more easily pronounced, PNI super-system. Whilst this may seem a rather baffling term, it actually describes an approach to medicine which seems innately logical to most people but until recent years, had no proven basis in medicine. Namely, that our biology and psychological states are intimately and irrevocably linked and between them, serve the vital role of developing and maintaining our health to ensure our survival. There are now a growing number of medical schools who have dedicated departments for the field of mind-body medicine, most notably the Cousins Center for Psychoneuroimmunology at the University of California. Steve Cole, an American biologist and pioneer in PNI research is a professor at the Cousins Center and was the subject of an article in *Nature*[3], heralding a sign that the scientific community are beginning to embrace this subject more openly. To begin to understand the PNI super-system, we first need to break the word down into its component parts: Psycho – the study of the psyche and our emotions; Neuro – our nervous system which constitutes our electrical wiring and messaging system; Immuno – our immune or defense system; Endocrinology – our hormonal or chemical messaging system. Whilst historically in medicine these have been treated as distinct areas of study, there is now growing research to prove that these systems are all intricately linked and are in fact interdependent, communicating through electrical and chemical 'cross-talk' in order to retain the finely tuned balance necessary for life, and affecting both our behavior and physiology.

Now we can see that the infrastructure is in place for our thoughts and emotions to directly affect our biology, let us return to the subject of our personalities or 'coping strategies'. For this we need to journey back to infancy to understand how our early experiences shape the way in which we will ultimately interact with the world and those around us and how this will also affect our ability to maintain health. I should just point out at this moment that I am not dismissing the very important effects of the chemical interaction between mother and infant *in utero*, but for the sake of time and space and the patience of the reader, I will be beginning at the cradle!

Human infants are entirely dependent upon their caregivers (usually their mother) for their survival; unlike most other mammals, which are able to walk soon after birth, they are unable to feed themselves or ambulate in their surroundings to avoid danger. This is a consequence of our being a bipedal species which requires a narrower pelvis for efficient locomotion, but which also necessarily restricts the size of the birth canal in females. Human infants, therefore, need to be born with a smaller head size than our mammalian cousins which results in a shorter gestation period and a comparative lack of brain development at birth. We are therefore wholly dependent on our caregiver for our survival, so it is vital that we maintain that attachment relationship at all costs. If the caregiver is either physically or emotionally unavailable, then infants will have to work to have their physical and emotional needs met which, according to Dr Maté, can lead to repression of pain and a need to protect the parent. By 'keeping quiet', the child ensures that the parent does not become stressed as this may lead to detachment: the child is therefore taking charge of maintaining the emotional equilibrium in the home environment, thereby reversing the normal child-parent roles. There are many variations of how this type of issue may manifest that are dependent on individual situations, but let us follow one hypothetical track as an illustration of the PNI super-system at work.

Let us take the example of an infant born to a mother who is under considerable emotional stress: perhaps she is bringing up the child alone without a support network and also having to work to provide an income. The mother's attention in this situation may well be understandably divided, and may not be wholly devoted to the infant. Her stress levels may make her prone to emotional outbursts which the infant may perceive as a threat to the attachment relationship. If an infant's cry for help provokes an outburst of anger from the mother, then it may soon learn that it would be best to suppress this behavior and in doing so, suppress its own needs. This may result in the child developing a tendency to repress his or her pain and anger in order to avoid rejection. This repression of emotions can lead to a situation where suppressed anger becomes directed at the self and, according to pioneering psychiatrist John Bowlby, famous for his work on Attachment Theory, this may also eventually result in 'inappropriate self criticism'[4] and a tendency towards perfectionism. If their emotional needs have been ignored, children may also develop a belief that they require no external help to take care of themselves, leading to a kind of forceful independence where they find it difficult to ask others for help. Denial of pain, a compulsive sense of duty, and a tendency to place the needs of others above their own are all correlates in adults who have experienced emotional abandonment in infancy. Here, we see the psyche (the 'P' of the PNI system), being molded by the child's emotional experiences.

The infant's developing biological and physiological states are also shaped by their interactions with caregivers. Emotions such as love, anger and fear serve to help children develop appropriate boundaries in their environment, to distinguish what is safe and what is dangerous, and this is usually developed under the attentive supervision of the caregiver. These boundaries must also be learned for our internal, physiological environment and it is the role of our immune system to manage this. Just as we need to learn who or what may threaten us externally, the immune system also needs to learn this distinction for the protection of the internal milieu. If the emotional boundaries with the caregiver have become blurred either through an absence of attention or conversely, through a smothering of attention where the child is unable to develop independence then, due to the cascades of neurological and chemical signals triggered by emotional responses, this blurring will also be reflected in the immune system's ability to mount an appropriate response. Our digestive system, or gut, serves as the gatekeeper to our internal environment deciding what is allowed in and what must be kept out. The digestive tract is a hollow tube, the contents of which is, technically, the external environment: we are built around a sliver of outside space and therefore the walls of this tube need to have strong defenses in order to protect us at a cellular level. The gut actually has its own nervous system, known as the enteric nervous system, which is independent and able to function without input from the brain or spinal cord – in a sense, the gut has its own brain, its own intelligence. However, it is also intricately linked to the brain via a neural network of connecting wires. This allows sensory information from the whole body to be relayed via the brain to the gut, and the gut to send information back to the brain and from there, to all the other sensory organs. This 'cross-talk' creates pathways which enable our gut to respond to our emotions and to our physical environment, and to mount an appropriate immune response when necessary. The enteric nervous system, with its independent intelligence, often responds faster than our conscious thought processes when faced with a threat, and the signals it sends to the brain and the rest of the body form what we know as our 'gut feelings'. We may try to rationalize a situation via our conscious mind, but the gut's signal is always authentic. If the child has learned to override the normal emotional responses in order to preserve the attachment relationship, and is therefore unable to distinguish between what is safe and what is dangerous, then these mixed messages will be reflected in the gut's ability to distinguish the same, potentially leading to reduced immunity. Here we see how the 'Neuro' and 'Immuno' portions of the PNI system interact.

The 'Endocrine' portion of the PNI system relates to our hormones, which are the chemical messengers acting as relays in the cascade of responses that allow us to adapt to our surroundings and mount appropriate defense responses without threatening our own physiological survival. This is a highly complex mechanism and well beyond the scope of this book to fully explain. Essentially, it allows for bodily resources to be sent where necessary (for example: blood to muscles when we need to fight or run), and pro- or anti- inflammatory chemicals to be mobilized to either fight an invading pathogen, or to mute an excessive inflammatory response. Inflammation is a vital tool for either attacking or containing invading microbes, but an excessive amount has a corrosive effect on our own body tissues. Hence, we need to balance this by producing anti-inflammatory substances to contain the response. This is a finely orchestrated mechanism which requires clear boundaries to be set for optimal functioning. When these boundaries are blurred due to our emotional conditioning, the signals become confused, and inappropriate physiological responses may ensue.

Anger is a tool we use to protect ourselves in the face of a threat. For instance, if we encounter a predator we need to display a show of anger in order to ward off a potential attack. This requires the cascade of chemical responses from the PNI system to fire up and thereafter, be burnt off in the expression of anger so as not to be left latent in the body. In the example of our infant, who learned not to display its anger but to repress it and turn it inwards, this may be reflected in the immune system mounting a defensive attack not on the external threat as it should, but on the body's own tissues. The child's outer demeanor remains calm and smiling, whilst the anger is deflected inside and the body chemistry runs unchecked. This is often correlated with a poor sense of self and the need to please everyone else in order to gain acceptance. This is not an uncommon finding in those suffering with auto-immune conditions where inflammatory chemicals secreted in response to a perceived threat and designed to attack invading pathogens are turned against the body's own tissues, such as our joints in the case of rheumatoid arthritis. This is summed up well by Dr Maté in his experience of working with patients suffering from this condition:

> ... the angry child got into trouble and experienced rejection. The anger and the rejection had to be deflected inside, against the self, in order to preserve the attachment relationship with the parent. That, in turn, leads to the "strong feelings of inadequacy and a poor self-concept" researchers have recognized in people with rheumatoid disease.[2, pp.172–3]

So, our infant has grown up and now we have an adult whom we may characterize as having perfectionist tendencies (John Bowlby's 'inappropriate self-criticism'), who never asks for help, who tends to hide any pain or discomfort, and who consistently puts the needs of others before her or his own. You may see these as 'personality traits', or perhaps now you may now see them as the mechanisms that the infant has developed to cope with its life's experiences.

So how does all this relate to authenticity? In our example, this compulsive need to help others in order to gain acceptance may lead to the person becoming surrounded by those who seek to take advantage of this trait and, consequently, this person may find that he or she is in constant demand to mop up other people's problems. This may well be at the expense of that person's own needs and even health, but she or he may be unable to express this outwardly – unable to mount a defense. This can lead to resentment and more inner turmoil. So this outwardly over-helpful person may be screaming inside, as she's just agreed to pick a friend up from the airport when she really needed the time to finish a vital piece of work for which she has a looming deadline. An authentic response would be to say "No, I'm afraid I'm too busy" but instead, she subjugates her own needs, says "Yes", and pretends that it is fine. The resentment she feels about this situation will be turned inwards and she may begin to develop uncomfortable symptoms, for instance in her digestive system or joints, as the inflammation of the repressed anger increases unchecked. When these emotional patterns have become engrained by repetition, they begin to seem so normal that the person is actually unaware of them, and therefore does not perceive them as a threat to health. If we fail to recognize a threat, we will fail to take action to remove ourselves from its path. I'm reminded of the analogy that if you throw a frog into a pan of boiling water, it will jump right out – it perceives the threat and takes action. However, if you place a frog into a pan of cold water and slowly heat it up, it will cook. It fails to notice the threat as it builds slowly over time and therefore, takes no action. So here, our adult example is 'playing the role' of being everyone's helper when he or she would really rather be the person who says "No": in this example, the person is not being authentic. When such patterns of behavior have become so entrenched, people are generally completely unaware of what they are doing, and therefore make no attempts to change them – they don't jump out of the pan.

Constantly playing a role is emotionally and physiologically stressful (although hopefully by now you will understand that these two categories are, in reality, indistinguishable). In the words of the great medical researcher Dr Hans Selye, who pioneered the concept of stress in the medical sense:

> most of our tensions and frustrations stem from compulsive needs
> to act the role of someone we are not.[1, p.405]

How many of us play a role in life in order to gain social acceptance or to suppress our innermost fears? How many people are attracted to the world of performing arts because one can spend a lifetime legitimately playing a part and being accepted for it? Do the performing arts represent a good place to hide for those trapped in this cycle?

To be truly authentic requires differentiation and autonomy. This is our ability to see ourselves as distinct beings and to have the independence and freedom to make our own choices without subjugating our needs to others. The less secure we are in ourselves and our relationships with others as a result of our emotional history, the more likely we are to relinquish some of our autonomy in order to maintain that relationship. This is not to say that we should shut ourselves off from emotional intimacy. In fact, emotional bonding is also very necessary for health, but like everything in the universe, there needs to be a balance. Being in any relationship, be it romantic, platonic or familial, where you are constantly subjugating your own needs to preserve the attachment, is every bit as perilous to your health as committing yourself to a life of lonely isolation.

Living in accordance with our core principles is also essential for health – not allowing ourselves to be drawn into situations which run counter to our beliefs and having the strength to say "No". Our body is usually very good at acting as an arbiter of these situations, sending us signs and signals to guide us towards the right decision for our health. However, most of us have either lost, or have never fully developed the ability to hear the body's warning cries – or choose to just plain ignore them. The headache we develop in a certain place of work, the queasy feeling in our stomach a certain person always seems to evoke in us – these should be ignored at our peril! Hence, the title of Dr Maté's book *When the Body Says No* – if you don't say "No", your body eventually will. It may begin with relatively small hints, but if the signs are not heeded, a much more dramatic response may be the body's only way to make itself heard. Small children and animals are usually pretty good about making their feelings clear, and removing themselves from situations in which they are not comfortable – if they don't like what they are being asked to do, they simply won't do it. This is what leads, in the film and theatre industries, to the warning "Never work with animals and small children" – they cannot be forced into an inauthentic experience which has nothing to do with either who they are or their own needs, and they are therefore deemed to be unpredictable. They neither know nor care if Spielberg is behind the camera; if they are tired, hungry, or bored, they will just let you know. However, as adults, we have become victims of our emotional and socio-cultural experiences and the hierarchical structure of a competitive world which can lead us to deem it 'inappropriate' to express our true feelings. We have lost the ability to be authentic and express our true needs. Pleasing Spielberg becomes way more important than pleasing ourselves.

When we deviate from these concepts of authenticity, we are likely to experience physiological stress driven by anxiety. If we perceive that we do not conform to what we believe others expect of us, then we become anxious that this relationship will be threatened. We somehow believe that the 'true' version of ourselves is not good enough and will lead to rejection so we create a new 'personality' which we anticipate will be better accepted. This may sometimes just happen on a transient basis. For instance, we 'play a role' whilst interacting with a particular social group because it seems the easiest thing to do at the time, but subsequently return to our true selves when back on home turf. However, in some cases this may be a much more engrained pattern resulting from childhood experiences and therefore 'encoded' into our biology. As such it is much harder to recognize and address, and is therefore potentially more threatening to our health. The role we are playing begins to take over until we are no longer in touch with our true self.

So what is happening when we experience anxiety and stress? Stress in and of itself does not have to be a negative event. Dr Hans Selye describes two types of stress, 'Eustress' – a positive type (as in eu-phoria) and 'Distress' – which is potentially harmful.[1,p.74] Both of these types of stress produce the same physiological responses, but eustress produces much less damage. Therefore, the external event which is causing the stress response (known as the stressor) is not the governing factor in our bodily reaction – it is the way in which we react to it emotionally. A paper cut (external stressor) on the finger of a tap dancer will be a minor inconvenience and unlikely to induce much anxiety, but on the left hand of a virtuoso violinist who will be performing to an audience of thousands that evening, it is likely to produce a potent stress response. Reverse the story, and place the cut on the sole of the foot and you get my drift!

A stressor can take many forms (an infected wound on the skin, food poisoning, or trouble with your boss at work), but they will all trigger a similar physiological mechanism – inflammatory chemicals may mount a defensive attack on the invaders to your skin or gut, or you may mount an emotional attack or defensive response towards your boss. This response could just be in a localized area (the wound on the skin), or body-wide if the infection has spread via the circulatory system. It is then necessary to recognize when the threat has been neutralized, when you are no longer in danger, so the system can be reset to normal. This ability to respond appropriately and then return to normal is known as our Adaptation Energy, which is a resource we are born with, but cannot be replaced. Hans Selye likens this to a bank account from which we can make withdrawals, but not deposits – so we should choose to withdraw wisely![1, p.428] Once this energy is used up, death occurs: we are no longer able to adapt to the stresses we face. We should also be aware of stressing one particular part of our body disproportionately. For instance, the pain a cellist may feel in the shoulder of his bowing arm after several hours of practice is a local stress response. This is a warning system telling him to stop using that body part and use another. Unless he is ambidextrous, then it won't be possible to swap his bow to the other side, but the message remains the same: stop what you're doing, and go and do something else. This is a local alarm response requiring localized rest of the affected area. However, if this cellist coincidentally has recently sprained his ankle and also has a general infection such as a cold or 'flu, the body will be fighting a battle on many fronts, producing localized sites of inflammation, and in this case he may need total body rest in order not to overwhelm the system. The shoulder pain from excessive practice may be the proverbial straw that breaks the camel's back. Repetitive tasks are damaging to the body and the body will send you messages when damage is imminent. This also, incidentally, applies to repetitive mental tasks – turning the same thought over and over until it festers. Hans Selye again:

> Nature loves variety . . . if you use the same parts of your body or mind over and over again, the only means Nature has to force you out of the groove is general (systemic) stress.[1, p.424]

Our bodies speak to us through the stress mechanism and we would do well to heed this advice.

I would also like to introduce here the concept of space in the context of both our physiology and music and movement. Our lives today can often feel so crammed with responsibilities and we find ourselves rushing from place to place to do what we need to do to make ends meet, whilst answering phone calls and being bombarded with electronic messages. This can have the effect of tightening our bodies through muscular tension and leaving us with an image of our body as being a densely packed, tightly wound coil. However, if we take a moment to delve into the sub-atomic depths of our physiology, the picture is rather different. Taking a peek into the quantum world requires that we suspend all conventional logic as, down here, the general laws of physics as we understand them break down. Everything in the known universe, including us, is made up of atoms – an awful lot of them! It is estimated that the average 70 kg person is composed of seven billion, billion, billion (or seven with 27 zeros after it) atoms and these things have been around for a very long time, being endlessly recycled. The wonderful author Bill Bryson in his book *A Short History of Nearly Everything* (a must-read for anyone wanting to know more about this stuff) says:

> Every atom you possess has almost certainly passed through several stars and been part of millions of organisms on its way to becoming you.[5, p.176]

He also suggests that, due to their endless redistribution, several billion of your atoms once belonged to the likes of Shakespeare and Beethoven – which might be a boost for the authenticity of those who perform their works! So these atoms are obviously extremely tiny: one ten millionth of a millimeter in fact. To illustrate this, I will borrow another analogy from Bill Bryson: if the Empire State Building were a millimeter high then, in comparison, an atom would be the thickness of a sheet of paper. If we now break this tiny atom apart, we see that it contains an even tinier nucleus made up of neutrons and protons.

However (if you're still with me, this is the bit I really want you to grasp!), this nucleus holds virtually all the atom's mass. The rest is just space. To get an idea of the relative sizes here, the leading physicist William H. Cropper describes the atom itself as being a hundred thousand times bigger than its nucleus, and the American scientist Ernest Lawrence famously compared the nucleus within the atom to a 'fly in a cathedral'.[6] So what this all means is that, at a sub-atomic level, the human body has more space than mass. If you just take a moment to really embody this notion, to visualize the concept that your body contains more space than solid matter, it can have a very powerful effect on releasing tension. It is an image I use myself, and one I share with my clients to help to unravel the knots and tangles we can often feel within our bodies. I am reminded of the words of the author Eckhart Tolle in his best-selling book *The Power of Now* on this very subject: ". . . even inside every atom there is mostly empty space. What is left is more of a vibrational frequency than particles of solid matter, more like a musical note".[7]

I love the image that the vast spaces in our bodies are humming with music, and this, perhaps, helps to explain why music has often been described as having powerful healing properties.

Likewise, the universe also contains much more space than mass (that's if you don't count the dark matter as mass, but that's a whole other book!). When we look up to the heavens or travel up there in a rocket, we say we are looking, or going into 'space'. Whilst this is often referred to as the 'empty vacuum of space', I think this creates the erroneous image that the term 'space' is analogous to 'nothing'. I prefer to believe that space is everything! Space provides context, and therefore meaning, for all that we see, hear, feel, do, and even are. Without it, most of what we know and understand would be meaningless: sounds cannot exist and would be meaningless without silence; the stars in the night sky are only beautiful because of the spaces that exist between them; the words we speak only make sense because of the gaps we leave between them. To bring this back to authenticity in performance, the space between the performer and the audience is the area in which the connection is made; it is in the space between the actor's words that understanding occurs; it is in the way that the dancer displaces the space around them that the movement is interpreted; it is in the relationship between the musician and their instrument that music is created; it is in the space between the musical notes that resonance is felt. As an Osteopath, I believe that it is the aforementioned space within our bodies which holds the potential for health, and much of my work is in supporting the body to dissolve the obstacles which can be created by tension and which serve to cut us off from this space. An injury can often cause performers to focus so intently on a particular body part, which not only emphasizes their pain, but moves them further away from the ability to be creatively expressive. I often ask musicians in my clinic to play their instrument in order for me to assess the body/instrument interface. The hollow space within the instrument is where the potential for sound is held and it is also where the sound reverberates: this is also true of the space within our bodies. When musicians wrap their bodies around their instrument the space is lost and the effect is to dampen or muffle the sound, just as if they had wrapped a blanket around it. When working with musicians, my approach to this issue is to ask that, as they play, they visualize the sound as passing through the space in their body and emanating from their back. Rather than focusing the sound forwards into the instrument, they allow it to fill the space behind them. This helps to open up the body posture, allows the sound to resonate through all the body's cavities, and serves not only to reduce their symptoms by off-loading the injured area, but also to change the tone and quality of the sound produced. The person, the instrument and the space all around reverberates with the sound and is often accompanied by a palpable change in the energy of the room. This leads to my contention that posture can be 'heard': I can hear if a musician is crowding the instrument and can visualize the accompanying posture without seeing it. I have often demonstrated this in group settings such as workshops and conferences, having a musician move from a crowded posture to an open one whilst playing. The usual result is that everyone in the room sits up, opens up their own body posture, and smiles as they hear and feel in their own bodies both the change in tone and in the general energy of the room. This is communication at its best, and is inherently authentic. It is what connects us to an audience, and we will delve further into this phenomenon in subsequent chapters.

There is so much that we don't know and never will know about the human body, but taking the time to understand just a few concepts which underlie our capacity for health can be an amazingly fulfilling and rewarding experience. As far back as ancient Greek times it was already recognized that the route to health was to 'know thyself'. The British cultural critic and poet, Matthew Arnold, writing in the nineteenth century, said:

> Resolve to be thyself: and know that he who finds himself, loses his misery.[8]

In our modern world we have explored vast expanses of our earthly and heavenly environment, and we have used scientific analysis to drive forward technology to extraordinary levels, but these external distractions appear to have drawn us further away from the ultimate human quest: to truly know ourselves. All the modern diseases which have stress as their underlying cause may be a very good reflection of this tendency to be distracted by the crazy, modern world around us and our need to find our place within its complex architecture, at the expense of a journey into our truly authentic selves which is the only true route to health.

Now that we have explored some of the concepts which may affect our health and their relationship to authenticity, in the next chapter we will explore how we can marry these concepts with life as a performer.

2

Being an authentic performer

Having explored the links between authenticity and health in the previous chapter, how does this relate to achieving authenticity as a performer? Actors spend much of their time playing roles and reading a writer's words, musicians are usually performing the work of a composer, dancers performing the work of a choreographer, so where does the authentic self of the performer fit into all this? Is it possible to play a role or wear a mask of performance and still retain your authenticity and, if you achieve this, does this necessarily limit the repertoire to which you are suited? There are differing thoughts about this within the various performing arts paradigms, with systems of training varying in their approach in how best to achieve authenticity. One notable example is the Method Acting technique, created by Constantin Stanislavsky and developed by Lee Strasberg, who formed the famous Actors Studio in New York which continues to produce some of America's most illustrious actors. This technique requires total immersion in a character and a drawing upon the personal emotional experiences of the actor in order to produce a convincing performance. However, some other schools of acting view this as a rather unnecessarily complex process and I'm reminded of the now famous quote by Sir Laurence Olivier, arguably one of the world's most talented and successful actors. When working with Dustin Hoffman on the set of the 1976 film *Marathon Man*, Hoffman, a Method actor and graduate of the Actors Studio, had stayed up for three nights without sleep in order to authentically mirror the experience of his character, who was scripted as "looking like he'd stayed up for three nights" and therefore arrived on set looking slightly the worse for wear. When Olivier questioned him as to why he looked so tired and Hoffman told him, he is quoted as saying "Try acting, dear boy . . . it's much easier"! We will be exploring the role of impersonation and mimicry in producing authenticity in Chapter 6, where we will also discuss the interplay between versatility and authenticity, but first we must begin by examining this breed we call 'performers'.

I have been surrounded my entire life by performers – my mother and sister were both dancers, my father a TV director and therefore, most of our family friends were also performers of one kind or another. I attended a full-time theatre school from the age of seven – a close-knit community of budding performers all jostling for a place in this coveted profession. From the age of eight, I began touring with a professional ballet company in a child role which I continued for the next five years, so I was seeing and experiencing the life of a professional performer first hand. After a fifteen year career in classical Ballet, musical theatre, stage and television acting and professional singing, I retrained as an Osteopath and now specialize in treating performers as well as still working as a professional singer with live bands. So when it comes to understanding the professional performer, I think I know the breed pretty well. As I begin to delve into what makes up a performing artist, I feel it necessary to clarify that I make these observations entirely without judgment – suffice it to say that it takes one to know one!

Even as a child, one thing that struck me in my interactions with performers is that the individual's performance was not necessarily restricted to the bounds of stage or screen. I often found myself wondering what these people, whom I 'knew' so well, were really like when no one else was there – when they did not have an audience. You have only to read the biographies of many famous performers to see that there is often a striking contrast between their public and private

18

personas – the face that they show to the world is not necessarily an authentic one. Sometimes, this may be a conscious decision in order to maintain some privacy, particularly if one is well known, but this may also be an unconscious process borne out of the issues of one's emotional history, as discussed in the previous chapter. The ability to recognize when someone is not displaying his or her authentic self is a vital tool in my osteopathic profession as I find the degree to which people 'perform' in their daily life has a direct correlation with their capacity to heal. The further removed they are from their true selves, the slower the body appears to respond.

So this raises the question to me of 'nature or nurture'. Does the training and career of performing artists cause them to move further from their authentic selves or is an inherent delusional personality an asset in this profession and therefore a process of positive selection? If a performer has learned from early experience that it is safer to hide behind a role they have created for themselves, do they have an increased ability to change their masks at will which lends itself well to this profession? As a child, I was a fairly good mimic and my impromptu performances were often rewarded with laughter and applause – this sort of positive attention can be highly addictive! As a youngster, I was actually painfully shy and tended to hide my real self from view, but I was perfectly happy to receive attention for my theatrical skills and therefore began to believe that this was where my true value lay. I began to define myself by what I could do, as opposed to who I was, and eventually the mask became the reality. I took my confidence from this mask, but rarely allowed anyone to look beneath it lest the reality failed to meet expectations.

An outwardly gregarious nature is often seen as an asset as a performer: after all, standing up in front of several thousand people and performing a highly complex task every night is not for the faint-hearted and would fill many non-performers with abject terror! But does this outward display of confidence mask a terrified individual within? I believe that in many cases this would prove to be true. It represents a dualism with which many performers will be familiar,

19

but does it actually serve a useful purpose in performance? From the masks of Comedy and Tragedy (the symbols of theatre from ancient Greece to the modern day), to the Pierrot of the Commedia Dell'Arte (the clown with a tear on his cheek), to the lyrics of Charlie Chaplin's *Smile* to Smokey Robinson's *Tears of a Clown*, there is a clear theme of dualism which I believe underlies not only all art, but the very nature of the universe itself.

The apparently solid nature of our bodies and all the objects around us is actually an illusion. Everything we are and everything around us is essentially just a buzzing mass of electrically charged particles. As we explored in the previous chapter, the atoms of which we are composed are no different from the atoms in the environment around us and, in simple terms, all the particles in the universe conform to a system of attraction and repulsion: they are either drawn together or they repel each other, a primitive mechanism essential to our reproduction and survival. What stops the particles that demarcate your body merging with those of the things around you is this act of repulsion. We actually never touch anything else, we electrically repel it – we don't stand or sit, we levitate! All the chemical and electrical 'cross-talk' which we examined in Chapter 1, functions by adhering to these elemental rules of attraction and repulsion. In the words of Hans Selye, nature can only answer 'yes' or 'no', so one needs to ask of her the right questions:

> She is not loquacious; she merely nods in the affirmative or in the negative.[1, p.19]

So at our very core, we have a duality. I want to clarify here that I am not referring to Cartesian Dualism – the theory of the seventeenth century French philosopher Rene Descartes, who propounded the notion that the mind and body are separate – which we now know is clearly not the case – but that there are opposing forces within our body and the entire universe of which we are a part, that require a necessary, reciprocal balance for optimal functioning.

This duality is also reflected in the structure of our brain and is explored by the psychiatrist and author, Iain McGilchrist, in his fascinating book *The Master and his Emissary: The Divided Brain and the Making of the Western World*[9] where he places the anatomy of the brain into the context of our social and cultural history, using references from music and art throughout history to explain its development. The brain has two cerebral hemispheres, the right and left, and each functions in quite a different way from the other. However, we are reliant on both in order to become balanced human beings and, like our PNI system, there is much cross-talk between the two hemispheres via the bundle of neural fibers known as the *Corpus Callosum*. The neurologist Marcel Kinsbourne[10] points to other oppositional pairings in neural structure which provide us with the necessary balance for function but, as over-simplification of this very complex and controversial area of anatomy can be misleading, I would just like to examine some limited aspects of this cerebral hemispheric dualism, which may help to illustrate some concepts relevant to this text.

In simple terms, our right hemisphere deals with new information, the left can only understand what it knows already, therefore making it a closed system. New information and new encounters, specifically with animate, living beings, will be presented first to the right hemisphere before being passed to the left for categorization and labeling. The left hemisphere is essentially our 'computer', adhering to a linear processing structure which views everything as component parts – it deals with abstractions and has a focused, narrow attention. Our right hemisphere takes the 'bird's eye view' and provides us with the necessary context – it has open attention and is vigilant to its surroundings. An example of the two hemispheres working in tandem is evident in our ability to be focused on a task like writing (left hemisphere) whilst remaining aware of our environment, for instance, if someone were to creep up on us (right hemisphere). The right hemisphere, with its contextualized view, sees the relationships between things, not just the things themselves (which is a left hemisphere trait), therefore it is the natural seat of music and movement which are by their very nature contextual. When we listen to music, it is our right hemisphere which responds. It also provides us with the embodiment of music, not just through movement, but through autonomic nervous system responses such as goosebumps, and changes in respiration or heart rate. These are mediated via the neural and chemical messaging systems we explored in the previous chapter. This is a good example of the mechanisms at work, whereby an emotional response to an external stimulus, such as hearing music, can create physical effects.

Although the left hemisphere typically deals with inanimate objects and tools, interestingly it is with our right hemisphere (which usually deals with animate beings such as people and animals) that we respond to musical instruments. Neurologically, we perceive them as animate objects, as having life. Most of the musicians I know would agree that they view their instruments as living beings – some even give them names. In my therapeutic work with musicians, I often note a breakdown in the relationship with the instrument when the musician is unable to play through injury – some cannot even bring themselves to open the instrument case because of the emotions this may elicit. Seeing the instrument is a sore reminder of their inability to play and, if the injury was incurred through playing, the instrument may even have become the object of blame. In these instances, an important part of the rehabilitation process is to rebuild the relationship with the instrument as if it were a living being. One needs to dissolve the emotional boundaries and reach a reconciliation before harmony can be restored.

However, whilst for an amateur or untrained musician music remains in the domain of the right hemisphere, professional musicians make more use of the left hemisphere. In order to become proficient in technical skill, the act of playing music needs to be broken down to its constituent parts and analyzed, which requires left hemispherical traits, before being reconstructed. It is essential, though, that it then be returned to the right hemisphere for expression and interpretation. If not, then what would be produced would be the musical equivalent of painting by numbers. Novice performers, who are applying mechanistic principles to their art form in order to learn, will often lack expression and interpretation – children learning new instruments usually just bash out the notes, which is never particularly pleasant on the ear! A study of professional musicians by Schlaug *et al* in 1995 [11] actually showed that the aforementioned Corpus Callosum, which is the mediator of interhemispheric communication, is larger in musicians who began training before the age of seven, than in non-musician controls. This suggests the increased need for this cross-talk in order to achieve musical proficiency. Although every individual makes use of both hemispheres, there are some who may lean towards one side or the other in some respects. I think we have all at some time heard musicians who are simply regurgitating the notes on the page, or seen dancers who are robotically reproducing the choreography – they may have become snagged by their left hemispheres! (Although this is a rather gross generalization of neural anatomy, I use it here for the purposes of analogy). Each performance should be a unique event mediated by the right hemisphere, not just a mechanistically regurgitated one – the performer needs to connect emotionally with the repertoire on every repetition. It is this uniqueness that represents the humanity and authenticity of art.

In our biomechanical system there is also a requirement for two-way action. For our joints to function and produce movement there needs to be a connection between two parts which allows for both separation and union. McGilchrist, when speaking of the muscle/tendon units which connect our joints, says that it allows the bones:

> to move away from one another and remain connected, or to move together and remain separate. [12, p.203]

Muscles also work in what are known as antagonistic pairs – as one muscle contracts, another allows for stretch whilst maintaining a slight counter-resistance. In order for optimal movement of a muscle, it needs something to pull against – something has to provide resistance for the action, or balance is lost. The body's systems are all inherently reciprocal and circulatory – a process of moving away and coming towards, attraction and repulsion, always requiring two parts.

So, here we have looked at some aspects of duality which are both necessary and required for anatomical and physiological function, but

I also feel that art itself shares this reciprocal duality. When we view a work of art, listen to music, or observe dance, it is not a one-sided process. The art does not just speak to us, it invites us to converse. It is a dialogue, not a monologue. Art requires the audience and the audience requires the art. A notable feature found in all art is a sense of longing or yearning, which is inherently reciprocal in nature, unlike wanting which is a linear movement towards a goal or target and is inherently one-sided. Longing has to involve both parties – a sense of a reciprocal connection that must be made. Wanting, on the other hand, requires no involvement of other parties and is innately one-sided. It is this reciprocal connection that draws us into any art form and serves to connect us with something other than ourselves, but to which we are somehow already intrinsically linked. There are so many examples of opposing forces that require such a connection in order to exist: the reciprocal tension of paired muscles is reflected in a dancer's pose, where an equal pull in opposing directions is essential for balance, thereby creating movement in the stillness; the counter-tension of the strings on an instrument producing the potential for sound; the opposing force of the bow as it moves on the strings; the dissonance which moves to consonance; the suspended chord which yearns to be resolved. All these reflect this circularity – a pulling apart and coming together, always in flow, always requiring each other and the context of the space in between.

Returning for a moment to the brain, you are probably aware that the left side of the body is controlled by the right cerebral hemisphere and vice versa. Many texts have made correlations with a dominance of right hemisphere traits in creative individuals, and calling someone 'right-brained' has become a colloquialism when referring to artistic types. As I mentioned before, this is a rather simplistic view and one that is contested by some neurologists and is the subject of continual study, but the following thoughts may provide an insight into how this mode of thinking may have developed. There have been several studies which show links with creativity and exceptional talents and a tendency for left-handedness (i.e. right hemisphere dominance).

One such study of musicians in professional orchestras by Chris McManus of University College, London found:

> a significantly greater proportion of talented left-handers, even among those who played instruments that seem designed for right-handers, such as violins.[12]

Artists are also often perceived as being 'moody' and prone to alternating periods of brooding and emotional outbursts. Although the issue of depressive illness and its connection to the right hemisphere is a complex one, there are many studies showing links between hyperactivity in the right hemisphere and depressive mood. In a study by Hecht, it was found that the right hemisphere is:

> . . . selectively involved in processing negative emotions, pessimistic thoughts and unconstructive thinking styles – all of which comprise the cognitive phenomenology of depression and in turn, contribute to the elevated anxiety, stress and pain associated with the illness.[13]

So this may be a further example of how artists have become labeled as 'right-brained'.

Melancholy, sadness, and the minor key in music are all again traits of the right hemisphere; joy and the major key are the domain of the left. Iain McGilchrist writes:

> It has been said that music, like poetry, is intrinsically sad . . . not, of course, that there isn't joyful music, but that even such music often appears to be joy torn from the teeth of sadness, a sort of holiday from the minor key.[9, p.73]

Again, here we see this concept of duality: joy is meaningless without sorrow, happiness meaningless without sadness. Each provides the context for the other.

If creative artists are seemingly so associated with their right hemisphere, are they then bound to have an underlying sadness – is it, in fact, a necessary part of being a performer? The neurologist Stavia Blunt, in her chapter on the Creative Brain in the text *Neurology of Music*,[14, p.36] says that certain stressors, such as early parental loss and childhood trauma, are actually conducive to creativity. So, is the issue of pretending to be someone you're not, this dualistic personality and an underlying sadness, representative of a yearning to reach out beyond one's current reality? Is it this yearning or longing that connects these types of people to the world of the arts and do they inherently respond to that implicit longing and melancholy so fundamental to music and artistic expression? If they had no experience of sorrow and longing, would that preclude them from producing an authentic performance? The neurological literature supports the close relationship of the creative brain with a variety of neuropsychiatric conditions such as depression: Stavia Blunt actually states that "the depressive experience is invaluable to the creative process."[14, p.43] We will explore the relationship between the creative brain and mood disorders further in the next chapter.

I believe that these emotional patterns and experiences can certainly be useful resources and potentially even necessary to draw from, either as an artist creating a new work, or in the interpretation and expression of another's work. However, for the preservation of health, I also believe that one needs to have an awareness of who one really is, and when one is deviating from one's true self. In my opinion, the people who are deluding *themselves* as well as those around them – those who quite literally believe their own press – are the people most at risk of suffering a disruption of their physiological balance, which may lead to ill health. A healthy realism must be preserved in order to maintain the equilibrium.

Today's cultural climate in the western world presents, to my mind, a huge challenge for the performing artist and the quest for authenticity. There has been a significant change in the relationship to the arts which has paralleled the global trend towards industrialization and mechanization in the last two hundred years or so. If we go back to our prehistoric roots, music is thought to have been our earliest form of communication, predating language by a long way. Professor Ian Cross of Cambridge University, whose work explores the biological and cultural bases for human musicality, suggests that:

> music, rather than simply being a complex sonic pattern produced and received for aesthetic or hedonic ends, can better be interpreted as a communicative medium complementary to language that is deeply embedded in, and that may be foundational in respect of, the species-specific human capacity to manage complex social relationships.[14, p.1]

Social bonding within a tribe is important for both our survival and evolution and, in our primitive ancestors, grooming through touch formed an essential part of this process. According to Iain McGilchrist, as social groups began to spread geographically, music became:

> a sort of grooming at a distance; no longer necessitating physical touch, but a body language all the same.[9, p.106]

It also served as a form of ritual to connect us with the spiritual world, to something other than ourselves, and the expression of music through dance was a natural embodiment of the sound. It promoted empathy within the group and sustained our intuitive connection with nature.

With the development of drama in ancient Greece, the human representations depicted by the actors enabled us to step back and view ourselves objectively, providing us with a context for our actions whilst also promoting an empathic response – again a reciprocal separation and drawing back in. Artists of all types tended to shun material wealth preferring to remain alone and connected with nature. It is only when we reach the Renaissance that we begin to see artists developing status, and the appearance of wealthy patrons of the arts. This is the beginning of art being seen as a commodity and a form of status and therefore power.

In the modern world we are arguably losing touch with the implicit nature of being in the world and see beauty as something to be acquired. We look at the visual arts with a critical eye and listen to music with a critical ear rather than allowing it to take us through to something

27

'other'. We are engaged in a monologue rather than a dialogue with it. Nietzsche had already become aware of this in 1878 when he wrote:

> The more the eye and the ear are capable of thought, the more they reach the boundary line where they become asensual.[15]

We have now created goal-posts for achievements in the arts which change the very foundational nature of their role in society. No longer just a reciprocal engagement with our tribe, we have created a system of targets, aims and rewards with which many true artists may find themselves at odds.

Another feature of the modern world is the increasing drive towards mechanization and viewing everything as a structural whole which can be broken down into constituent parts. When we encounter something that prevents us from using this methodical approach – something which cannot be described by language alone, something which is so much more than the sum of its parts – we have a tendency to be suspicious, dismissive or even disparaging of it. Lack of ability to explain things should not negate them. One of my own personal favorite quotes is attributed to the poet William Cowper, that: "absence of proof is not proof of absence".[16] Even Einstein, despite existing in the world of science, said that:

> the fairest thing we can experience is the mysterious. It is the fundamental emotion which stands at the cradle of true art and true science.[17]

The indescribability of the innate 'other-worldliness' to which the arts connect us is, I believe, its most powerful quality. Any attempt to attach intellectual understanding to it simply misses the point.

This mechanistic view leads us to believe that anyone is capable of producing what were previously believed to be innate, in-born talents. If we can just follow the easy six-step program, we can all write music like Bach – just find the formula, add water and bingo! This acquisitive, linear processing inevitably leads to competition – we are turning art into a sport. We not only want to know 'how' to get there, but also 'how fast?' The value of a slow honing of skills over time is replaced with a race to the finishing line. The advent of celebrity culture is helping to drive this as we consistently elevate performers to the roles of heroes, who apparently live lives to which we all (potentially rather foolishly) aspire. This is an illusion rarely borne out by reality, and one based on very shaky foundations.

The increasing fragmentation of both the nuclear family and wider communities, through a rise in urbanization, coupled with the increasing need to travel beyond our social groups for work, has led, I believe, to the increased need to connect vicariously with others via the medium of film and television. We replace our chat over the garden fence with a daily soap opera, and begin to identify ourselves first with the characters and eventually, the actors on our screens. Then we start to elevate the actors to a god-like status who, through the power that this public attention affords, can then command ever higher salaries, often resulting in ostentatious displays of this wealth. This is driving the celebrity culture, and now we not only identify ourselves with the characters portrayed on screen, but begin to follow the actors' lives themselves via the media and gossip columns. This, in turn, drives them to promote a public image of themselves which may be far from authentic. The aspiration is to 'have what they have' and the reciprocity of art is lost as we pursue this more voyeuristic approach – we don't 'look', we 'stare'.

So, what happens to performing artists who become 'famous'? How do they retain their authenticity? What drives some well known artists to turn to addictions or destructive behavior patterns? Does the act of becoming famous create this, or is it an innate tendency developed from early emotional and physiological experiences, which is then just tipped over the edge by the freedom and excesses which celebrity, and the concomitant financial freedom, can bring? Are the very traits which made them so successful as performers also the cause of their own downfall?

We discussed the nature of the arts as being intrinsically a bonding mechanism for the social group, but when a musician is elevated to the status of virtuoso, or a dancer is plucked from the shared dressing room of the corps de ballet and placed in a single room with a star on the door, they are necessarily being removed from their 'tribe'. They may seek to retain their ties with the group, but inherently the dynamic has changed and relationships are irrevocably altered. If this happens early in childhood, then it may have an even stronger impact.

I can illustrate this with a personal story. Although on a relatively small scale, I did experience some focused attention for my performance skills as a child, which had a profound effect on my social interactions and certainly affected my behavior through to adulthood. As I mentioned before, as a very tiny eight year-old, I was chosen from a group of much older children to play a child role in the London Festival Ballet's production of *La Sylphide*. This involved performing quite complex choreography whilst being partnered by one of the principal male dancers, and necessarily brought me much attention in the dance world at the time. For the next five years I would be performing up to four London seasons each year, as well as both national and international tours which periodically took me away from my regular schooling and therefore, my peer group. Each time I returned to school from a tour, I experienced a degree of rejection from some of my peers who would exclude me from such things as a newly formed social clique, or a new group activity, blaming my exclusion on the fact that I was always 'away on tour'. I soon learned that having professional success made me unpopular and resulted in exclusion from the social group. I began to correlate being successful with punishment, even associating it with a sense of shame, something that followed me throughout my career and is still with me today. I can remember distinct times in my past where I have actually sabotaged my own progress or played down my achievements for fear of rejection from the social group. Expressing my true, authentic self seemed to trigger an innate fear of abandonment. Although I am now aware of this tendency and have spent time exploring the reasons behind it, I still have to check my responses and actions very carefully to avoid subjugating myself, and therefore my health, by falling back into the traps of my old behavior and quashing my natural expression.

My experiences were on a very minor scale, so it makes me wonder how on earth one would cope if such success were on a global scale, where it is not only the behavior of your own peer group that may become altered, but the behavior towards you of the population at large. When you have a public relations (PR) machine creating and disseminating an image of you to the general public, which may be far removed from reality, how do you remain authentic? Can you become lost in the gap between who you intrinsically are, and the image of you which is being portrayed?

For some insight on these issues, I have turned to my good friend and colleague, Paul Roberts, who spent fifteen years as the lead singer of the well-known British punk-rock band *The Stranglers*. When Paul joined the band in 1990, they were already highly successful and he was taking over from the existing frontman, Hugh Cornwell, who had also written many of their hits. Gaining acceptance from the existing fan base and media would prove to be extremely challenging as, inevitably, comparisons would be drawn with the out-going singer who was a much loved figure in the pop world. I first met Paul about five years ago when I was singing with a large UK function band and my then male singing partner had had to leave the band at short notice. Paul stepped in at the last minute (about three hours before the show) and we hit it off instantly. I connected straight away with his boundless energy but was equally thrilled to find that he was every bit as obsessive as I was about detail! We spent two hours going through the set list with a fine toothcomb, before plowing straight into a 35-song gig together. After one night, I felt like I'd been working with him forever – we just seemed to implicitly know what each other was thinking. We then continued to work together for the next four years and I now consider him one of my closest friends. When I began writing this book, Paul very generously offered to share his experiences of fronting a globally successful band and how he coped with the issues of fame. This took the form of a long 'chat' and I have included his thoughts verbatim in narrative form to retain the essence of his contribution. My questions and comments are in italics.

When you have a PR machine creating an image of you to the public, how do you remain true to yourself, or can you?

I think that probably, fundamental to all this scenario, is that you have to remember who you are, who your friends are, what it is that means the most to you. I think that can kind of get you through that situation. I don't know what it would be like to be going through this at 19 – a friend of mine from Hollywood, he was a child star and he's never recovered. But there again, there are innate issues within your personality – it's a question of whether they exacerbate your state of mind or your personality or they don't. Or is it actually the situation that's making it happen? There's an impression of me out there that I have to constantly not push away, but I have to gently persuade everyone that that's not my way of being, but it doesn't break down the public perception of what the PR company is doing. To a certain extent really you have to be prostituted and let them do what they like to represent you to sell their records to pay you.

Did you have any input in how your image was put out there? Were you involved in that process or did it just happen separately?

Well, it's assumed. I joined a band that already had an image, so that's a different thing. You adhere to it, but all of *my* fans, all of the fans of 'me', (rather than the band), they know who I am. They say "you always talk to us, you're a nice guy". They all understand that I'm a very giving person, they absolutely 'got' me. My mother tells me that I've never changed since I was a child. I know I went through a change when I first got into it, because you definitely live in that idiom. But at the same time, I didn't want to be known as a notorious punk rock thug – I didn't want to be known as that because it's too much. All I ever wanted to be known for, really, was performing and being a reasonable performer, or pleasing people, or satisfying them or making them feel good. I didn't really need a PR machine, but you need a PR machine because PR is stronger than talent. PR is all-encompassing. Everything is done with PR. I grew up in the 60s, I watched *The Beatles*, I watched Buddy Holly, I watched all these people on TV and in recordings – but there were more pioneers then. What's happened is that people look for anywhere that you can earn money on this planet and they think "how can we make it into a nice little box that we can sell very easily and not have it all so wild and all over the place?". I remember a guy at EMI was talking about the fashion. Yes, you always had that with *The Beatles*, you had that with certain acts of course, you always had sex appeal, but it wasn't so powered by PR. It came to the point where you could write a song and go actually, "I've just realised I can rely on this PR" and some of the artists do. So much is just a PR lie and then people believe it. I've worked with people who believed in their own press and that really worried me. It's a really difficult question because PR's got nothing to do with reality, I don't think. It's like the internet: with certain tags, with certain key words you can get your business everywhere. Your business could have been non-existent the week before. Then there are those reality shows which are apparently about singers. It's entertainment, I dig it, that's fine, but I just don't need the insult of being told by someone who's making 20 million pounds a week that it's *about* singers, because it's not. I don't mind you making your show – we had *Stars In Their Eyes*, *Opportunity Knocks*, that's all that these modern reality shows are, but it's been blown up and it's got a lot more money behind it. That's the ultimate PR.

So do you think that you managed to retain your sense of self through all of your experiences?

I did to a certain degree, you know. But you do become 'cock of the walk' for a while, about who you are. If I was very honest about myself, as a man in his 50s, I know what I've done, where I've been, who I've affected, why I've affected them and I think I'm a good bloke. And with that, and remembering all the goodness in my life and all the good people and the love and just the good times that you can have when you're real, it saved me. And also probably the age that I got into the business – I was 30 when I joined *The Stranglers*. I'd been through a lot already. I was a drug addict when I was a teenager, I'm still a registered addict, so I went through stuff in my struggle to grow into being an artist of whatever sort. I mean initially, I wanted to be a producer, that's what I wanted to do. So I think it's about believing yourself or believing your own press. The first thing you do is you try and re-examine what you're doing, to improve on it or at least not get into a rut.

Do you think that it stagnates the writing process as well when you're distanced from your sense of self?

Absolutely yeah, it just destroys it. You can't work. "Oh I've had 18 hits like this" – well so what? I don't think you're going to get a 19th! You need to change. You'll look through a catalogue and you will see that. Bobby Darrin's a great example where he played and sang so many different genres and he sung them all really well. But I wouldn't really want to be a young guy in the PR thing now. Now it's all perfect, it's all perfectly packaged and the minute someone has an inch of success, bang – they're everywhere. And it's just wrong, it's wrong for all of us, but definitely wrong for *that* person. And I love the kids – I met all the *Take That*'s when I was going through my thing – *Spice Girls*, very sweet. But the public have got no idea about what they're bowing down to and no idea of the effect it's going to have on those young people, of course they don't. The singers on the receiving end need to be able to filter that stuff and I don't know how easy that is when you're inside it. All I know is that you have to be a company man, there is a point when you're a company man – if that involves you playing up to the PR, then great. I got asked by my manager to go on a late night TV chat show and start a fight once. I've never felt more physically, mentally and emotionally confused and I just thought this is the most ridiculous thing I've ever heard. Why do I have to prove that I'm hard because I'm in this band – that's the element, you know, misogynistic and hard core – well that's not me. So the last thing you want is your PR machine driving that. But I don't embrace all that and I don't have to – that's the short answer. I didn't like that you were expected to have that portrayal of being a hard case. My toughness comes from my existence and I really feel that, I really don't bend towards anybody.

Did you find that this was a struggle at times, that you were wrestling with your conscience?

Sometimes, you just go, "I don't want to do this, but I've got to do it". The toughest thing was banter on stage, when I thought "I don't really know how I'm going to approach this" or how I'm going to deal with it, because I'd had this intellectual person, Hugh [Cornwell] before me and I can't really live up to that – I have a different kind of intellect. And then I thought, well that's me and it takes you a while to get that. If you've got a strong intellect and personality, it will definitely punch its way through. I've got that now, where I've heard all these other people telling you how or what to do, but actually, when I work, relax and come out of myself, that is what makes my performance. That's me, that's my PR. A lot of people say to me "You are a great entertainer", "You're a performer", which I love . . . and I am turning into one! I'm so happy and relaxed about what I'm doing that I have turned into one and it's my life, every minute of the day now.

How does fame affect your relationships with family and friends?

Well it almost starts from when you just get on stage, it's not even about being known: when you get on stage, you've suddenly separated yourself from the existence that your friends probably want you to have or you've suddenly moved outside of your remit as a friend. I had some dramatic changes to my relationships – awful, really awful. One of the first people was a very close friend – we were all doing drugs up to our eyeballs, heroin, injecting and all sorts of stuff – at the point when I got out of everything and didn't want to know, she sort of said, "You don't really care about us anymore." I do care but there's nothing I can do anymore and that was a kind of real 'eureka' moment for me. At that point, I had just got on stage as well – I think it was a bit of jealousy on her part, a bit of anger, of lack of wanting me to move away or change and maybe I was a driving personality in that relationship and that circle of friends. And I remember thinking, there and then, that it's not me that's changed – someone said to me, "You've changed," but I went, "No, no, no, I haven't changed, you've changed your attitude towards me because you can't deal with the fact that I'm two foot higher than everyone else on a stinking, beer-stained stage, waltzing around with these four blokes in a van, freezing my backside off for no money" – what's that got to do with being clever? I just had to do it and I haven't changed, I'm still a show-off, I love it, but I hope it just comes across alright. But my family was amazing. I love to include people, I want them all there, all the time. They loved it and my friends got to know that. But there was a bitter falling out with one of my best friends. I guess I was being a bit arrogant at the time – I was going through my bubble that I went through for a year. It ended up going into violence and to this day it's still there. He made a complaint about me not inviting him backstage when other people were and he didn't get a pass, but it was out of my hands. It's just really tough because I used to say to him that all I want to do is come to your house and have a cup of tea and talk about the football – that's what I want to do.

Do you think if you hadn't joined the band, would that stuff have still have happened? Was that fundamentally there?

Yeah – I think it was there. It was actually a great help that I got into rock and roll because it brought it to the surface – it burst that boil. It's like anything – you must not want revenge, you must not want these things because they are so unhealthy. I know people who still dig the fire about what we did – but you've got to let it go. I know it sounds easy, but you've got to go through this problem, but it will end. But if you keep looking back, it will begin again.

Did you find that you acquired other 'so-called' friends – did you find that people attached themselves to you for superficial reasons because of your position?

One of them attached themselves rather well, with a knife! I always remember when we used to have backstage do's, the first people I wanted to see were my parents, my girlfriend and my son, which meant so much. There was another girl used to follow me around. This woman came to London, but expected me to give myself over to her all the time – this is what people expect, it's massive. I have had so much of this – this woman recently tried to get hold of me on Facebook. The last gig I remember doing with the band was in London at Shepherd's Bush, she was waiting for me, but I didn't want to know, I didn't want to talk to her. Every time I saw her she would grab my arm and sniffle and cry. I've had many other situations like that and people writing to me about having cancer and dying. Another fan saw me going out the back of a gig and said that her friend was in tears because I wouldn't see her. I said that I didn't feel well and I'm thinking "I have to explain myself to all of you all of the time and I'm sick of it – why can't I have a night off?" Victoria

Wood said in an interview on TV that she goes outside after a show for photographs and people say, "Be funny, do something" – and she replies that "I've just given you an hour and a half of me, I can't give you any more". That's exactly how I felt. When I was with the band, the energy that used to come out of me – people used to say that that's not true, it's false – but they don't know anything about me. Do you think I could do that every night if it was fake? I might be insanely ill and hyperactive and something else, but that's why I do that, maybe I love it – maybe I need to do that because I think I'm going to die tomorrow so that's why I do it – it's my last statement on earth.

Do you think that this is part of the issue of art becoming a commodity, that people somehow have a right over you and own you to a certain extent?

There's the commercial aspect, they buy your records so you deserve to pay lip service to them. When you're appearing somewhere, it seems that you've got all day (you might not have all day, that's what they don't realise – sometimes you're holed up in a hotel doing interviews non-stop). If you've got the time and you come out and there's a crowd of people, by duty you should attend to those people – you may not want to, but they've bought your records. That's one aspect of it. The actual spiritual, emotional aspect of it, I think, is irrelevant: it's a nonsense, it's stupid, it's a terrible human trait, it's weakness – the thinking that the whole idea of God is that you can put your problems onto someone else. I am not God and I don't need your problems – I do feel for you, but I can't help you. John Lennon had that guy who appeared in his garden, and then one day a guy appeared outside his flat and killed him. It doesn't matter how famous you are, stuff like that happens.

Is it not the fact that people 'think' they know you and may have an issue with you that makes you a target?

I used to get beaten up for wearing a bright blue shirt and skin-tight leather trousers, people used to beat me up, so I don't know. I don't think it's the preserve of entertainers, I think it can happen in real life. I think fame just makes it easier for those sick people: they're obsessive, they're weird, they've got big issues in their lives that, bless them, they can't deal with – it doesn't make them the worst people on the planet, it just means I don't want them near me. I've had those people near me and it's very scary. People make comments because you do things, of course they do. I watch my mother going through the papers and saying "bloody idiot" and I'm always defending people, going "You don't really know them, you don't know what they do or what they don't do." I'm a performer and I know what it's like. I can't even stay and see people I really, really love after the show to say hello to because I just want to go home. I stand on stage now and say to the audience "Well you're staying up all night, but I'm going home to feed my cats" – that's what I say to them and they love it! When you get a 15-page letter from a nutcase who's been sectioned 27 times, you certainly start going [whistles] – I need to get a milk-round! Very scary. 48 phone calls on one night, just because I offered someone a cup of tea. Every night I could see her from downstage and I'm thinking "Oo – she's going to get me tonight!" Another one whom I've never even met in my life wrote me a 15-page letter about "our love".

Do you think being famous made any destructive behaviour patterns you may have had any worse?

I don't think so. I mean occasionally, when you had the chance and the time was right, you would trash something because that's all there was you could do really to show your anger without starting a fist-fight with someone. I tried to start a few fights, certainly with members of my band, and I hit an audience member once. But all the drug-taking had happened before I joined the band. One of the reasons I stopped doing everything else in my life is because I did get a break, I did get paid to play. It's all I ever wanted to do. So it's a really long thread going back to my childhood. That's all I ever wanted to do so everything I did that was negative, was because I wasn't doing what I wanted to do.

So do you think that joining the band and getting appreciated for what you do actually saved you in a way?

Yes. My girlfriend, bless her, because I fell in love with her and just finally doing it. I used to have a friend who I kind of really looked up to in Chiswick, very well known on the London Blues scene, he was an inspiration quite simply. He was the only guy in Chiswick that was doing music really, he was a lovely guy, still a friend, and I always thought "I want to be like you". He came round once and said "Have you got any gear?" and I said "Sorry mate, don't have anything like that" and he said "I can't go on without it". That was a key moment, it really was. I never forgot and I thought "I don't want to do that". I did drink a bit on the American tour, but it worked for me because I just let everything go. Bashed it out and people loved it. I think you're certainly in a position where you can abuse anything. The first time I came back from tour, I realised that there was a void. That was a problem – that was the biggest issue. I then made the judgement that a lot of these young bands have never done what I did as a teenager, they didn't do the drugs, the girls and the drink – I did all that. I did a lot of stuff in my teens for some reason. I've done the other stuff, now I just want to do the music. All these other guys, they're doing the music so they can have the drugs, have the drink, have the girls. Then I thought it really makes sense that when you come home and you've got to make your own bed, you've got to tidy your own clothes and you have got someone in your life that says, "That's your stuff, you deal with it", then you start to go, "Oo – that other stuff isn't life". I kind of realised that very quickly, which is probably why I only spent a year being an idiot. Someone like Robbie Williams, he grew up with this stardom and he's a great entertainer – he's a good kid really. I hear so much of me in him when he speaks. As performers, we're exactly the same: unbounded energy, this guy is wired, he's out there – that was me. I heard him recently talking on the radio about his new song, then he started talking about his kid and he started crying and I'm thinking "That's me, that's me". I certainly identify with the way he is, he's so honest. Yes, he's been called an idiot by loads of people, but I'm going "He's a kid." He has actually now come out and said "I'm an entertainer, I'm not Kurt Cobain, or any of those guys." It's the same thing about having money – does that free you up? Anything that puts you above other people, or on a pedestal that people worship, gives you the freedom. In this world, money gives you freedom, but it also puts you in jail. It also creates terrible situations in your life where you will open doors that you will never close. You've got to be so strong to close them. I've done that. The emotions you go through when you're touring, you're like an open wound.

When the relationship with your fellow musicians breaks down, how do you continue to produce authentic music and performances?

I don't think you can. You're totally living your own life, your living your own thought processes, you want to create your own thing, you don't want that label any more. What happened to me was, I didn't think there was any creativity left in the band. So how can you work like that? How can anybody work like that? I wanted to continue what we were doing. I wanted to work on songs, I wanted to play music. I enjoy sharing that with people, that's what I find pleasurable about it, because you learn, and then you create something great. But when you're working with people, it's kind of like being suspicious of your partner – the things you fear in other people are your own thoughts. It's that simple. So that's what happened, it broke down, irreparably. It broke down very quickly and I just wasn't prepared to write blueprints, I wanted to take the band on with the same attitude and do something – I wanted us all to be ourselves. The very idea that you can be a druggie or drinker and have a focussed career is ridiculous to me. So yes I used those tools, but only for inspiration, occasionally. Then the rest of it: 10% inspiration, 90% perspiration, that's how I worked. That's how I used to write my own records. But then I had clear lucid approaches for the initial ideas as well. So apart from using drugs and drink to come up with ideas, I also did it without that, but those ideas always developed, all of them. But I felt that the band didn't want to come with me, I felt I was always going with them, even when I didn't like what we were doing, so that's wrong as well. So physically, I became in pain because mentally I was screwed. I couldn't work like that.

When you made the choice to leave the band, had you just reached the point of no return? Was it affecting your health?

Absolutely, it was affecting my health. I'd given everything I had all the time to them, all of the time. I was probably wildly stressed out for years – it was bugging me for a long, long time and I was doing that for 16 years. And that is a long time. And then I did my last gigs with them: we had a terrible weekend away, I crashed my car, I turned my car over on the motorway. The whole thing was that I was probably going to kill myself eventually, which I nearly did. I remember doing very odd things that weekend, Nottingham Rock City it was. I walked off stage and I told one of the fans I'd had enough.

I come to the junction of the M 25 and M 23 and the next thing I know I was upside down and inside out.

Had you at that point made a decision to leave, or not?

I think I had, yeah. I was just, you know, life was difficult because I didn't have any money. I was just getting a retainer every week, but it was tough to know what the hell I was going to do and there had to be a point where I was going to have to worry about my future, with no money. But what keeps my feet on the ground, it's what probably saved my life, is I just had to think "How am I going to do this?" I didn't know how to do it, I had to think it all through and I thought, well if I don't go now, and I wait another three or four years, and we still won't make enough money for me to see my future out, what's going to happen then? So I had a word with the manager. He gave me an ultimatum to buck up my ideas and get in line with everyone or I'll have to go. I went "I think I'll go, because I'm not putting up with this anymore." I said, "I don't want to be an alcoholic, I don't want to drink all night. I tell you what then, I'm leaving."

As it happens, my whole life has been about stepping stones and I don't know if it's fundamental to my existence, whether I had to be a musician. I think it was definitely what I wanted to do but I want good experiences in my life. So all the things I've done, I've enjoyed and I've done with gusto. And *The Stranglers* was never going to be something that I did for ever. I had better options, like a life. It was really tough for years. It's still tough – you don't want to look online at anything, you don't to look at people slagging you off, who don't even know you. A guy destroyed my Wikipedia page. I found it so amusing but it also really distresses you, not that it might make others think badly of you – it's distressing that human beings have got the ability to be so cruel. That's what really worries me. I hide. I don't like being noticed too much – I do like it but I don't.

When that person did that, I thought "Is he going to be knocking at my door?" I lived like that for years on end, I still live like that. I still live with the fear of someone knocking on my door and just doing something about it. It's not so bad now. I nearly moved out of Brighton because I heard someone playing live versions of *Stranglers* stuff because someone told them where I lived – unbelievable. That's scary – it's still there all of that. It really isn't a problem now, but back then it really was. I can't stand the thought of people having my phone number, I can't stand it when I get strange texts – that freaks me out, it genuinely freaks me out to the point where I go "Change the locks, change everything – phone numbers." Well, I'm not doing that.

So it taps into a paranoia? Do you think that paranoia was always in you prior to The Stranglers *or because of it?*

I might have had a bit of that. You know for a fact when you watch John Lennon get shot dead that that could happen to you – not necessarily that it's going to be a piece of lead in your belly or in your head, but something equally unsavoury – anyone invading your privacy. This is my home and if someone wants to come to the door, they'd better fight me to get in – I'm not going to be attacked.

So you've had to build defences to protect yourself

Yeah. But I used to get picked on when I was a kid for being blonde and blue-eyed – I used to get threats and beatings.

So the fame, the notoriety, sort of exaggerates what's already there?

Possibly. I don't know how deep that is, if it's too deep, if it's too analytical. The person who wants to be a rockstar, probably has a little bit of a strange chip in their head, as is someone who's going to spend ten years of their childhood learning to play the violin. But you're dealing with someone who's got issues already and I probably did have issues, I don't know. But a lot of the people in the arts are affected, politicians are affected. The other thing is, with this crazy process, it's unique in the point where you have to believe that what you're doing is 100% good for mankind – you're benefitting someone. You're doing something that's great. You're putting something out there – you're making a statement in this world. But then you'd better get yourself some sandbags . . . and a brick wall! I really do believe that artists find each other and you all suffer together really, you suffer the same stuff. You say "I'm an artist", "I'm a musician", "I'm a performer" – you don't have to say any more. It's wonderful when it's wonderful, but when it's not, it's not so good. You've got to have strength. If you're strong enough to be in the business, your skin's got to be so tough. I work with different people all the time – most people work with the same people 30 or 40 years, they don't change their lives every week. So you've got to be thick skinned – that will carry you through the other issues that are attached to it. You don't want to ever be that pop star. I found it funny when someone took the mick because I was wearing a bow tie and singing *Fly Me To The Moon*. At least I'm not wearing a *Triumph* T-shirt and jeans at 60, pretending I'm rocking out when actually I'm living on the past. I think that's a bit more painful, actually.

I love rock music, I love writing – I want to write, but I'm not stupid enough to spend my life wasting those months, years because, my god, how many years have I got left? 30 years? I want to enjoy myself – I don't want to keep worrying about being great – I've got 60 songs which are great – I've done that, sitting and listening to them. I've had EMI telling me that the songs are so great, but they can't market them. "Why not if they're so great?" Don't keep ringing me up: someone who I would have cut my right arm off to talk to was phoning me saying how great my music was but they can't market it and it was driving me mad – so I don't want to live like that.

So, is not the process of writing and creating something enough? There needs to be an appreciation of it externally for it to have legs?

Well, I think you've got to have an appreciation of it because, otherwise, you could do anything: you could tell yourself anything was great and become more and more marginalised – in fact, become a hermit and go crazy. That's literally to say that what I'm doing is worthwhile – that's not to say that you're great. The other aspect of it is, being pragmatic, that you need to earn a living in this world. So what's the point of wasting your time doing something creative if you're not earning a living when actually you should be feeding yourself, you should be feeding your family, you should be looking after business. I've got friends who are still 'artists' and they're moaning about being poor – I don't want to be an artist who has to moan about being poor. I've had to postpone my creative pursuits within the songwriting situation and music, to live and be happy. It's not the yellow brick road writing music or songs or anything artistic – it's something you have to do, you are compelled to do it. I still write in my head, but I know that I won't be able to live if I can't pay my rent – I can't write and have a studio: "He was a tramp, didn't he write good stuff?" – I don't want to do that. I'm more practical than that, but I know I could sit down tomorrow and write if I had the time – I'm trying to make the time to get back to it. I'm a working class guy, but I'm not an idiot. I need to have a roof over my head. What are you going to do if you turn up to a publisher in your shoeless feet and go "I've got some songs" . . . "Yeah, right – bins are round the back"!

If you had your time again, would you do Stranglers *again, knowing what you know now?*

Knowing what I know? [Sucks in breath.] Well, I don't really regret things, I know that's a cliche . . . I do regret a few things. I'm at the time of my life now when it's very easy to have so many opinions and to say so many things, to be so 'clever' and knowledgable and intellectual about it all. I would probably go and study and get a proper job! I had my 50th birthday a few years ago and nearly 90 of my friends turned up – it just said so much to me. But I've never been able to be there for my friends and you know how much I value my family. Reality means a lot to me because I've lived outside it. When I said I was leaving [the band], my girlfriend looked at me and cried and I said "Just trust me, just trust me – I don't care what I have to do, I'll do it, don't worry". She was just in tears – she's never questioned me about what I do, she has never put a barrier in front of me, she has never, ever, ever, ever done that. Seriously, I don't want to be out at night all the time when my friends are around – I don't want to be around in the day. It's like being a millionaire, you've got all this time to play with, but everyone else is working. I got paid everyday even though I didn't work. People would follow you round the supermarket going "You're Paul Roberts" – I suppose I've never not been 'on duty'. I think I'm normal and everyone else around me is weird!

I imagine that before all of this, you would probably have always been a pretty extrovert kind of person so do you think you found a natural place for that as opposed to the experience having created it?

I found a career that I could dump all of my stuff in and it's acceptable. But I don't feel uncomfortable, I feel really great. The greatest compliments to me are when people notice what I do for other people which goes back to pleasing people. My father loved to watch people dance, he didn't want to dance himself, he just loved watching people enjoying themselves – I love that.

It seems like you're always wanting to belong – to be a part of a tribe. So much of what happens in the arts seems to separate you from that.

Yes, it does. You're still part of another tribe but you know what, when they're working, you're working. You have a laugh, but you're constantly on your own. There comes a point when you may be talking, laughing etc. but then you have to focus – I'll go and find a toilet, find anywhere to be alone and focus on what I've got to do, that's the biggest thing. I heard a story recently from a journalist about a huge Hollywood star who, in his dressing room, was a small, hunched-up old man but as he followed him out to the stage, as he got nearer and nearer the wing, this guy just grew . . . and I do it all the time. I love including people, that's just one of my traits, I love people to share.

So that tallies with what you were saying about writing, when I asked why you can't write for writing's sake. So you're doing it to include and share.

Yeah – to share and to give people something – *which is what art should be.* Yeah – it should certainly create a reaction – if art's not created a reaction, then it's not art. Even if someone hates it, it's created a reaction – or they're ambivalent, you know. I became ambivalent to the British artists – I just thought, "What are you doing here?" *The Unmade Bed*, Tracey Emin – I don't really get it. Definitely it's got to create a reaction. Now we've got all this facile stuff, we've got all these people hooking onto stuff – it just is rubbish. It's selling magazines, newspapers, TV news, adverts, it's selling all the stuff that you don't need. You don't need it, you need to have your own thought process. You need to go through stuff yourself and I know everyone can't do that, but it really is how I live. It's simple. You include someone, you communicate with them, you understand them, well you can do that to your own life. If one person in my life looks at me and decides that mine is a good life, then good. I do have all the processes of anger, hate, revenge but I lose them very quickly because actually, it's so much nicer. And I have been severely tested.

Do you think you needed the experiences you've had to teach you the lessons that have created the person you are today?

I don't know really. I have never changed, I still feel that I can feel how I felt when I was a child. So I'm not really sure if it did – it probably got something out of my system. I travelled the whole world and that is something that I'm grateful for but no one person has helped me – it always goes back to my self-belief and my drive even though I'm still waiting for someone to go "I've sussed you out", "You're not very good really". I'm an entertainer, I'm cool with that, but I'm not a nasty guy, I'm not spiteful, I don't do that other stuff.

Do you think if you had had a 'normal job', if you hadn't had that outlet for your creativity, do you think that would have changed you.

It's tough when you've got all these years behind you. I always thought that if I'd have got a lot of money, I'd have gone off the rails – definitely. I'm an addictive personality. I got a lot of energy out of my system, I've got a lot of bottled up energy. In that respect, it was probably a good thing – I don't think I'd have been built for the office, I probably would have killed someone! All of my energy would have gone into killing the guy opposite me! I've always had tenacity. My father brought me up saying "Don't ever rely on other people, don't ever bor-row money, don't ever be in debt." These are very strong influ-ences in my life. I think I feel really quite relaxed at the moment because I know I've got my rent paid for this whole year and I've got half the rent paid for next year. I don't want to rely on that, but I feel so good about that. In that respect, I've always had more money at the end of the year since I left the band. Since 2006, I got through two and a half years with band money and royalties. And then I started having a real bad time, but then it started to go up. It's been pretty good – work's really hard but, anything I can do to earn a living . . . I think there are very few people that do what I do who've been privileged like me, who have been in scenarios that you would never have dreamt of in your life. I've dreamed about military machines all my life and then I got asked to go up in a Hercules – they flew a Tornado bomber across my head – how many people does that happen to? I dreamt about that when I was a little kid – soldiers and stuff like that. I was on an America's Cup boat as 16th man – you have to pay 20 grand for that if you're in the business – I blagged my way in because I let someone into a gig! These things! It's endless – everything I've done, I've packed it in. That is what that has given me. I know that a lot of it sounds material but it's not about that – I wanted to see the world. I grew up never thinking I'd get on an aeroplane, yet, through my own perseverance, tenacity and absolute insistence, I got there. And now I'm still singing and I'm loving it. I love singing, singing, singing. And being there. I love it when people like it because I love them to be joyful, I love to see their faces and think "They really enjoyed that." They love it and they can't get enough and then you go home on your own! You sit there and watch the football and have food and a smoke and that's great. Three years ago when I was doing a show, I sat in my house and thought "Life is perfect." I said that out loud – "Everything is perfect." I've done so much – I'm sitting here, I've got a sold-out show that I invented with someone, I've done this, I did that – I really said that. And now I'm filling all the places I've never been. I've just got back from Africa – how did that happen? All the bits I've never done in the world are getting filled in by working on a cruise, and I'm getting two and a half grand a week – not very often! It's just incredible – I don't know how

I got there. I don't know how I got to the point where people just say "You're a great entertainer." I don't get that, don't get it at all. But I know I do it and I'm not bad!

_____

This is a wonderfully frank account from someone who has truly experienced the full spectrum of the good and bad within the performing arts and I think his words sum up the extremes at which so many performers live. His has really been a career of extreme highs and extreme lows, but what shines through it all is his absolute passion for his craft and the immense joy he draws from sharing this with an audience. After four years of working together, I can personally vouch for the effect his magnetic energy has on an audience and I was never happier than when we were sharing a stage. Such a connection with the audience is a true echo of the wonderful reciprocity of art which should always be a symbiotic experience. However, maintaining one's balance as a performer when one is living at such extremes can be a difficult thing to achieve. In the next chapter, we will be exploring the physiology behind creativity and how this can manifest in both the physical and psychological pain a performer can sometimes experience.

3

Creativity and sensitivity: the physical manifestations

In this chapter we will be exploring the biological relationship between creativity, which could be said to be an innate prerequisite for being a performing artist, and our physiology, with particular reference to the pain and discomfort often experienced by performers in the pursuit of their craft. There are, of course, some rather obvious reasons why performers may be experiencing pain – the awkward postures required to play certain musical instruments, the hours of repetitive practice, the extreme range of movements involved in dance – all of which can push the body to the limits of tolerance. However, I also believe that there is another layer to the symptomatology in this population which is tied up with some of the concepts that we have previously explored.

To be creative requires sensitivity. To be a dancer, one requires an acute awareness of one's body for finely tuned balance and placement; to be an instrumentalist, one requires an acute sense of hearing and touch for the instrument interface; to be a vocalist, one requires a fine control of the vocal and respiratory mechanisms. It could be argued that the more creative a person is, the more sensitive he or she will necessarily be. However, this may also result in a heightened response to stressful stimuli in their environment. The Pulitzer and Nobel Prize winning author Pearl S. Buck said of creativity:

> The truly creative mind in any field is no more than this: A human creature born abnormally, inhumanly sensitive. To him ... a touch is a blow, a sound is a noise, a misfortune is a tragedy, a joy is an ecstasy, a friend is a lover, a lover is a god, and failure is death. Add to this cruelly delicate organism the overpowering necessity to create, create, create – so that without the creating of music or poetry or books or buildings or something of meaning, his very breath is cut off from him. He must create, must pour out creation. By some strange, unknown, inward urgency he is not really alive unless he is creating.[18]

I'm sure some, if not all of this will resonate with creative artists, who often tend to have a hyper-awareness of, and therefore sensitivity to, the world around them. This may be reflected in the physical response to a pain stressor, or equally to the emotional response to one's social environment. It is ironic then how the profession of being a performer, which necessarily requires a high level of creativity (and therefore sensitivity), is highly physically demanding and also routinely lays you open to the criticism of both your peers and your wider audience – highly stressful on both accounts!

One of the things I find most interesting and intriguing when treating performers is how they respond to and cope with the experience of pain, as this can often be dichotomous. If we follow the above train of thought that creative people are necessarily highly sensitive, then one would expect that this would be reflected in a heightened response to pain in the tissues of their bodies. Indeed, in my experience of treating performers using manual therapy, I generally tend to find a hyper-reactivity in the soft tissues, necessitating a much lighter touch in order not to create post-treatment discomfort – a little goes a long way. Conversely, however, many performers, particularly amongst the dancer population, experience pain as an everyday occurrence and even perceive it as a normal part of their profession. "No pain, no gain" is a firmly entrenched mantra in many cases. They are often able to tolerate a high degree of pain for prolonged periods and some will even wear this as a badge of honor, martyring themselves for the sake of another well-worn mantra "The show must go on". It is not uncommon that by the time performers come to see me with their symptoms they will have often been enduring high levels of pain for prolonged periods. They will often only make the decision to seek help once their symptoms begin to seriously interfere with their ability to perform their craft, if not having forced them to stop completely. This commonly results in a much more complex scenario in terms of treatment and rehabilitation, which potentially leads to a longer recovery time. By ignoring the body's early warning signs, as discussed in the previous chapters, this often results in performers being the authors of their own misfortune.

So what are the physiological processes behind the pain we experience? Many of the performers whom I treat have very little understanding of these and I believe that this lack of knowledge in itself can contribute to the overall pain picture. Any mystery surrounding the performers' symptoms increases the anxiety they are experiencing which can cause amplification of the perceived pain. Once I have explained to a patient the mechanism behind their pain this often serves to reduce the anxiety, and consequently the pain, making treatment more comfortable. Another source of anxiety can stem from diagnostic terms about which performers often hear, either via the professional grapevine or the ubiquitous internet. Some of these terms seem to have attained quite mythological status amongst performers and are seen as 'Diagnoses of Doom' – examples being tendinitis and carpal tunnel syndrome. Again, reassurances that neither tendinitis nor carpal tunnel syndrome is a fatal condition, and is eminently treatable, serves to reduce the stress response to more proportional levels. Much of the research literature on stress cites lack of information as one of the most potent stressors to our bodies, which then leads to the physiological changes we have already explored via the PNI system. So, in the interest of reducing any potential anxiety in those who have chosen to read this text, I will describe here some of the reasons behind the types of pain that one may periodically experience.

Although I am against the notion that the human body can be reduced to a series of measurable parts which can be used to explain this incredibly complex entity which constitutes a person (as with art, I believe it is the parts of us which defy analysis that give us our greatest qualities), I will use some basic analogies here for the purposes of clarity and simplicity. We will start with muscle pain as it is one of the most common issues experienced by performers in the pursuit of their craft. If we compare our muscles to an engine, we can see the following similarities: for normal function they require a fuel supply in the form of oxygen, in the presence of which a combustion process takes place to provide the necessary energy for action (e.g. a contraction of the muscle) and, as a result, waste products are produced. The oxygen molecule necessary for this process will have originally arrived in the lungs via an intake of breath. In order to reach the target muscle, it will have jumped into a waiting taxi (a hemoglobin molecule) which then runs it via a series of ever branching tunnels (our arterial and blood capillary system) to eventually arrive at its destination (the target muscle). After the combustion process, the ensuing waste products need to be removed via another series of vessels, namely our venous and lymphatic systems, to be eliminated from the body or recycled. The muscle is richly supplied with these vessels for fuel delivery and waste excretion. The cyclical motion of contraction and relaxation associated with normal muscle movement helps by acting as a pump for these fluid systems, in addition to the pumping action of the heart. However, if we take the example of a muscle in the left forearm of a violinist with sub-optimal playing posture, we see this muscle being asked to do many things at once: to hold the arm in the air whilst countering the weight of the instrument, both of which require a static contraction force, and to then produce quick dexterous movements of the fingers, which requires dynamic contraction capability. Most muscles are designed to favor either one or other of these types of contraction (static or dynamic) but not to do both at once. If you add to this the fact that these contrasting movements are also potentially occurring in a slightly twisted orientation, as the arm wraps around the instrument, this places the muscle fibers in a compromised position resulting in sub-optimal output. All this is a good recipe for muscle overload which is likely to result in the muscle becoming short and tight. This tightening and twisting has the effect of choking off the aforementioned vessels which deal with delivery and drainage. Although the oxygen supply may be compromised by this situation, if activity is still required the muscle is able to continue functioning by switching to another system of combustion known as anaerobic (without oxygen) respiration. However, this alternate system tends to produce more waste products and if the drainage system is also backing up, due to the vessels being squeezed, this may lead to an accumulation of such chemical waste. To continue to work without oxygen can be potentially damaging for the muscle and will cause it to fatigue more quickly, therefore the body will trigger an immediate pain response to alert you to this fact. This is known as 'ischemic' pain and is the same pain experienced by a heart attack victim when the heart muscle is being starved of its oxygen supply. It is also the pain you feel when you have been carrying a heavy bag for a while and which usually induces you to swap hands. The body is telling you to stop contracting this muscle and allow it to re-perfuse with blood. Sometimes, however, pain may be experienced some time after activity has ceased and may even take several hours to appear. This is usually due to the build-up of the aforementioned chemical waste within the muscle which hasn't been able to drain away, and also potentially from the metabolic waste that is the usual result of local tissue damage. These waste products act as a chemical irritant to the nerve endings in the muscle which is itself a cause of pain. Additionally, the build-up of this waste may also cause distension of the muscle tissue, stretching the surrounding fascial sheath to a potentially harmful extent, so once again our ever vigilant body produces an alarm signal, in the form of pain, to alert you to this situation. This type of pain, which appears several hours after exercise or sometimes the next day, is known as delayed onset muscle soreness or the 'DOMS'. All this is a rather simplistic description of complex physiological mechanisms, but hopefully it has been helpful to illustrate some of these basic processes.

Another way that a muscle can become damaged, and therefore produce pain, is via either a direct or indirect trauma. A direct trauma is where a muscle is damaged via an external force – perhaps you fall onto the muscle causing bruising or something collides with you. An indirect trauma is where the damage occurs due either to a muscle overload or overstretch. One of the most taxing things for a muscle and a potential cause of overload is something called an 'eccentric' contraction which involves the muscle both contracting and being stretched at the same time. An example of this is holding a heavy book in your hand and placing it down on a table – the muscles which bend the elbow will be contracting to counter the weight of the book, but, as you lower it down, they will also be being stretched whilst still controlling the rate of descent with a resisting contraction. If the muscle is at the same time twisted or is lacking in the necessary strength, damage can occur. Overstretch occurs when the attaching points of a muscle are forcefully pulled apart or pulled beyond their normal range, particularly if the muscle is also cold at the time. An example of this could be a dancer who launches into the splits before having warmed the muscles up. In these scenarios, there is usually frank damage to the muscle fibers which can be labeled in many different ways – a muscle strain, a muscle tear, a pulled muscle, a ruptured muscle. With the exception of the latter, these terms are interchangeable and all imply that the muscle fibers have been torn to some extent. These tears may be at a microscopic level, and therefore barely discernable, through to a more significant disruption of fibers which will likely cause discomfort. A muscle rupture implies that the whole muscle has become detached from one of its connecting surfaces or has become completely severed in the middle – thankfully, this is quite rare! The issue with any degree of tearing is that, as the muscle is richly perfused with blood vessels in order to provide the requisite fuel supply, any disruption of the muscle fibers will result in a leak of the blood and other fluids contained within it. We can liken this to the example of a cut on the skin: the skin fibers are disrupted, fluids leak out and the body's response is to 'plug the leak' to avoid a dangerous loss of fluids. On the skin, this is achieved by the formation of a scab and much the same thing occurs within the muscle, where it is called an adhesion. This is a quick-fix response to avoid leakage of precious fluids but, as for the scab on the skin, the adhesion does not behave in the same way as the surrounding tissue. It is hard and inelastic and therefore can affect the overall contraction and stretch capability of the muscle as a whole. A significant sized adhesion, if left unchecked, may eventually form into something called scar tissue. This is a permanent area of compromised tissue which reduces the overall elasticity of the muscle, thereby increasing the risk of further damage, as well as having a negative effect on its overall function. Treatment with manual therapy serves to address these adhesions first by breaking them down and then by stimulating optimal fiber reorientation during the healing phase, thereby returning the muscle to full function. Correction of the posture or behavior that may have led to the damage in the first place must also be addressed in order to prevent reinjury.

Another factor in the production and experience of pain is related to the level of stress or anxiety that the person may be under at the time and the resulting response of the sympathetic nervous system (SNS). This is one of our body systems that is under automatic (or autonomic) control, meaning it requires no conscious will for its activation. The physiologic stress response is a complex system which is beyond the scope of this book to explore in full, but I will just highlight here some aspects of it which can relate to the perception of pain. The SNS is one of the systems involved in the 'fight or flight' response – a primitive survival mechanism enabling us to defend ourselves against a predator or to make a quick escape. When under such a threat, it is vital that all our senses are aroused in order for us to fully evaluate the situation. So, our system is flooded with hormones, such as cortisol and adrenaline, which serve to heighten those senses as well as increasing our heart rate and sending blood coursing to our muscles to ready us for action. I'm sure we have all seen animals, such as our household pets, in this situation at one time or another – eyes bright and gleaming, ears pricked, hackles rising, muscles primed – they see, hear and feel everything around them. If you were to reach out and touch the animal in this state, you are likely to receive an exaggerated response – even a light touch will be received in an amplified way. When one is in this state of arousal it may therefore take much less provocation to trigger a pain response. The perception of pain is also likely to be amplified or exaggerated by such a heightening of the senses. This is not to say that the person experiencing this pain is consciously exaggerating or making it up, their symptoms are absolutely real. Dr Hans Selye, in his research on stress, showed that there are also measurable increases in muscle tension during times of stress which can cause pain, particularly in the neck and back.[1, p.176] However, any symptoms need to be viewed in the context of the person's state of mind, as the level of pain being experienced may not directly correlate with the level of actual tissue damage. We have already discussed some of the ways in which the world of the performing arts can be anxiety-producing, where one is constantly exposed to criticism and lack of autonomy, so is it any wonder that this population will tend to have increased sensitivity to pain? Whilst it is thankfully rare these days to find oneself in a situation of mortal threat, our primitive mind does not discriminate – fear is fear and the physiological response is the same. The more information the performer who is experiencing pain has about these mechanisms, for instance by placing their pain in the context of their current stress levels, the more the anxiety can be alleviated. Such reassurance, as we have seen, helps to 'dial down' the pain response to more manageable levels. Understanding that the perception of pain is not always directly correlated to the level of tissue damage can often be very encouraging: just because a particular area of the body is extremely painful does not always mean that the underlying damage is as dramatic as the symptoms may make it appear.

Conversely, however, there are times when this fight or flight mechanism can actually dampen our perception of pain (I made no promises that this would be simple!). When you are in a situation of mortal threat, pain may be a distraction that you can ill-afford when your survival is at stake. The cascade of hormones produced in this state include some that have anti-inflammatory properties (such as cortisol), that can actually switch off an inflammatory process whilst we are in our aroused state. Examples of this exist in the literature from the First World War, where there are reports of soldiers in the trenches who experienced severe injuries, such as severed limbs, but were unaware of their severity at the time. Some were even able to get themselves out of the danger area despite these disabling injuries. It was only once they had managed to get themselves to relative safety, and someone had pointed out that they were missing a limb, that they noticed the injury and only then experienced the pain. If they had been made aware of their pain at the time of the injury, they would have been overwhelmed and unable to remove themselves from the danger. The body is intelligent enough to know that it can survive without a limb but it wouldn't survive the inevitable further attacks if it remained in the danger zone. Therefore, the pain response was suppressed until the mortal threat was no longer present. My own grandfather experienced this very phenomenon whilst fighting in the Gallipoli Campaign: his legs were struck by shrapnel which shattered both his femurs but, at the time, he felt no pain. He recalled that he couldn't understand why he was unable to stand or walk, but could see that both his feet were lying at very strange angles. He was borne away on a stretcher, the middle of a convoy of three stretchers, when two high-explosive shells struck the ground either side of him. Of the convoy, only he and his front stretcher-bearer survived, his rear stretcher-bearer and all the others were obliterated. This remaining soldier then dragged him to the first aid station behind the lines and it was only on this jolting ride, where he had to grip the sides of the stretcher to prevent himself from falling, that my grandfather began to feel the pain of his injuries. Once they reached safety, the soldier saluted my grandfather and said "You'll be alright now, sir," and disappeared. He never found out this soldier's name and was therefore never able to thank him. I never met my grandfather as he died before I was born, but he apparently rarely spoke about his experiences during the war. However, on one singular occasion, he shared this story with my father and I am therefore grateful to him for allowing me a small glimpse into the life of this brave man and his personal experience of this particular quirk of our pain perception mechanism.

History is littered with reports of people performing almost super-human feats in moments of great danger, either to save themselves or others, and being oblivious to any associated pain. However, this mechanism can also be in play when the threat is not mortal, or where there may even be no such threat at all. If we remind ourselves of Dr Hans Selye's description of Distress and Eustress having the same physiological results,[1,p.74] this mechanism can be apparent also in times of euphoria, for example, when a performer is in the 'zone' of a performance. Most performers, myself included, will have had experience of this when they were perhaps either nursing an injury, or one had been incurred during a performance, but had no perception of the pain whilst they were on stage. In the theatre world this phenomenon is known as 'Dr Footlights'. When performers are wondering how they can possibly perform that evening, due to pain or feeling unwell with a cold or a stomach problem, the usual mantra they chant to themselves, (or is repeated to them by their fellow performers), is "Don't worry, Dr Footlights will get you through." This is an example of the buzz of hormones being produced, albeit in a positive sense in this situation, but having the same effect of damping the pain response as it did for the soldiers. This, however, can be a dangerous situation where, by abusing this mechanism, we suppress an important warning sign from our body which may lead to our causing ourselves further damage. It has the same effect as blocking the pain with a strong analgesic. We would also be making those withdrawals from our adaptation energy account which cannot be replaced. The body contains its own amazing intrinsic pharmacy, but we can abuse it and become just as addicted to it as we can to extrinsic drug use!

I mentioned there the so-called 'zone' of performance which is a phenomenon that is well-documented not only in the field of the performing arts, but also in the sports world. This is a usually small window of time when performers or athletes feel completely at one with their craft and where almost no conscious thought is necessary for their actions. Some report that they feel almost disembodied from their actions, becoming observers of their own performance, as if the body had a mind of its own. Perhaps we can relate this to the concept of the right hemisphere of the brain being allowed its freedom of expression without the machinations of the left hemisphere. Remembering that the right hemisphere gives us the 'bird's eye view', seeing the whole picture in context, may help to explain the performers' sense of perspective when in the 'zone'. The left hemisphere traits clearly need to be present, but they are no longer dominating those of the right. Rather, they are in harmony with them. What is interesting is that many performers report that when they are in this state, there is a notable lack of tension in the body. The movements come with ease and the body no longer has to contrive the necessary shapes, but becomes purely a conduit of the creative expression. However, this state or 'zone' is also all too often fleeting and elusive. By its very definition, it cannot be consciously willed and therefore any attempts to recreate it will be likely to fail. Once we begin to try to deconstruct and analyze it, we will have necessarily passed it to our left hemisphere where it simply cannot exist: it is beyond the limits of language to describe. The 'zone' is, by its nature, an abstraction which therefore means that it requires belief, but will defy proof. In trying to describe it, we will surely destroy it as it cannot exist under a microscope: it is the rainbow which we know exists, but we cannot grasp and any attempts to reach it will simply move it further away. With my performer patients, I often try to encourage a defocusing of the mechanistic aspects of their skills: for musicians, this will sometimes involve 'playing' their repertoire without either their instrument or even physical movement. I ask them to 'think' a particular piece and sense how this feels within their bodies, then just extend that sense via the arms (or legs) to the instrument. For dancers, I use similar concepts of imagery, first visualizing and 'feeling' the choreography and then progressing to movement borne as an extension of this thought process. I add to this the suggestion that they not focus on the shapes their bodies are creating, but rather how their body movements displace the space around them. These concepts serve to remove the focus from a site of pain or injury and to reduce the amount of tension produced by the movements. I also believe that by encouraging this mode of thinking, which allows the right hemisphere free reign, this will create more potential for reaching that elusive 'zone'.

Returning to the concept of stress and anxiety, whilst we have seen previously that lack of control or lack of information can trigger the hormonal cascade of the stress response, this can also be triggered by a sense of feeling unloved. Therefore, feeling nurtured, appreciated and regaining one's sense of control would then be the antithesis of this response, serving to suppress this stress reaction. The world of the performing arts is often an uncertain one in which a performer has to deal with regular experiences of rejection. As many performers' personal identity is tied to their professional abilities, this repeated rejection can lead to a sense of not being appreciated or loved as a person. Conversely, however, the buzz of a highly enthusiastic audience showing their appreciation for your skill can likewise be interpreted as a display of personal love and affection which can become highly addictive. If you only ever feel loved and appreciated on the stage, then you can start to feel lost and alone anywhere else. When you add to this the flush of adrenaline which tends to accompany performance, this can add to the attraction of the performance state. Adrenaline can be a highly addictive drug but, like other mood enhancers, can also leave you with a slump when it abates. Hence, for the performer, the stage can begin to represent personal appreciation and elation of mood, whilst the 'real world' can start to seem a very lonely place. Loneliness and isolation are also known to be potent stressors, so we can see here how performers may find themselves in a cycle of inflammatory reactions which can begin to have a destructive effect on their health.

Inflammation is a very necessary part of both our defense and healing systems. We produce an inflammatory response to fight off invading microbes and to promote healing of our own body tissues. The anti-inflammatory hormones we produce are there to keep this system in check and to ensure the response is proportional. Too much inflammation would have a destructive effect on our own body tissues, such as in the case of auto-immune diseases like Rheumatoid Arthritis where the body begins to attack its own joint surfaces. Therefore we need to have a finely orchestrated balance in these pro- and anti-inflammatory chemicals in order to preserve and protect our own tissues. This balance is conducted by the brain and spinal cord, which react to the stimuli and stressors around us, and orchestrate a response throughout the body via the PNI system. The fight or flight mechanism, mentioned above, is designed for occasional use in the event of extreme situations: it facilitates the mounting of an appropriate response and then resets the system to normal once the threat has been eliminated. However, in today's modern world, we often find ourselves in a perpetual state of stress, where the threat is mainly more psychological in nature, and this can result in a loss of balance of this finely tuned system. This is known as chronic stress and is characterized by an abnormal production of the anti-inflammatory hormone, cortisol. As we have seen, this has the effect of dampening our inflammatory response, which can also lead to a dampening of pain signals, meaning that a greater degree of damage is required to produce a pain response. The body elevates the pain thresholds so any tissue damage has to reach more significant levels before symptoms are experienced. This is a similar mechanism to that experienced by our First World War soldiers, even though the threat in this case is a non-mortal one – the body doesn't discriminate. With the inflammatory response so muted, this can allow invading microbes to spread dangerously unchecked around the body, which may eventually overwhelm our defenses. For example, a small cut on the skin may have allowed a bacterial microbe to enter the body, but a local inflammatory response would have dealt with it at the point of entry and neutralized the threat. However, if the body is flooded with anti-inflammatory chemicals due to chronic stress, the local defense mechanism may be rendered impotent, allowing the microbe freedom to roam and potentially overwhelm our system. Here we can see how chronic stress driven by psychological and emotional factors can have a negative effect on our immune system.

This is all an over-simplification of very complex mechanisms, but I think it is useful to understand that the pain of an injury has so many components which must be explored and addressed for optimal healing to occur. Whilst some injuries are unavoidable – accidents will occasionally happen – many of the performers' overuse-type injuries could be avoided, or at least minimized, through a better understanding of the mechanisms involved in tissue damage, as well as the role that stress and anxiety can play in overall health. Pain is a great teacher and the more 'in tune' you are with the signals the body provides, the better protected you will be.

So now we have an understanding of some of the mechanisms involved in the production of pain, let us return to the issue of performers who deny their pain. Some of this tendency can be put down to purely practical needs: if one is earning a living from one's craft, taking time out to rest a painful body may have negative financial implications in terms of lost earnings. The potential cost of treatment may also be a factor for struggling performers, which may lead to their ignoring their pain in favor of protecting their bank account. Much of the performance industry is a close-knit community of freelance artists where the 'bush telegraph' is a well-entrenched phenomenon: so if you are known to be suffering an injury, word may soon spread that you are not fit for hire. Even within the apparent security of a large dance company or orchestra, where treatment may be freely available and paid for by management, a conflict of interests can be set up which may still lead to the negating of injury on the part of the performer. If management is paying for treatment, then they are usually privy to what would normally be confidential information known just to the patient and therapist. Being seen going in and out of the therapy department by management and co-workers also makes confidentiality almost impossible. Therefore, if a new production is being cast or promotions being considered, then performers may not wish news of their injury to be public knowledge lest it lead to their being considered unfit and therefore being overlooked. So, they ignore the pain and struggle on rather than face any apparent rejection: they subjugate their needs for an externally-driven goal. This is a precarious, short-sighted choice where more serious injury and therefore job security is risked: the higher one builds the House of Cards, the more dramatic will be the fall.

However, I also believe that this denial of pain stems from something deeper within the performer's psyche (and therefore physiology) which may have been created by early childhood experiences and positively reinforced by training. We have already explored the issues of early emotional abandonment leading to the repression of pain, and also how these phenomena may be a factor in the development of creative individuals, but what is it about the specific journey of the creative child to an adult performer that contributes to the denial of pain? The role of teachers and parents in the training pathways of young performers will be examined in more detail in subsequent chapters, but we need to highlight here the nature of much of the performing arts training culture. I refer particularly here to the training of both the classical dancer and classical musician, as these two groups usually require training to start from a very young age and arguably require the highest devotion of training hours to accomplish professional proficiency. Therefore these disciplines have potentially the greatest capacity to shape the physiology of the developing child. In my experience, it is rare to meet a professional performer in either of these disciplines who has not be trained under the banner of 'no pain, no gain'. Students are sometimes told that they will not 'make it' as a professional performer unless they pay the price in blood, sweat and tears. They are constantly reminded that they are entering a world where 'only the strong survive' and many teachers display their own battle scars with pride as evidence for this. This produces a culture where pain is expected, experienced and then repressed and rewards are often given for doing so. I recall a particular incident in my own dance training at my college end-of-year performance when I was about 17 years old. I was one of three soloists performing an excerpt from the ballet *Paquita* and shortly before the first performance, both the two other soloists sustained injuries which prevented them from performing. I was also suffering an injury myself (which may lead you to question our rehearsal schedule that this should have occurred to all three of us simultaneously!), but my injury was considered to be of a lesser nature in that I could still dance, albeit whilst enduring a degree of pain. As we had no understudies, it was decided that I should take on all three solo roles, which I had to learn at 24 hours notice. I managed to get through the performance by taking large amounts of pain killers (and with a little help from 'Dr Footlights'!) which, although they temporarily masked my symptoms, unsurprisingly resulted in an exacerbation of my pre-existing injury. So here I was clearly putting my own physical health (and potentially my future career) in jeopardy for the sake of a college performance, a risk that most rational people would consider not worth taking. However, the response I received from my teachers, peers and the audience was one of much congratulation and back-slapping for my brave and heroic behavior in upholding the age-old mantra 'the show must go on'. This is a clear example of how the repression of pain and subjugation of one's own needs are highly rewarded in the culture of the performing arts and I certainly relished the positive attention and 'applause' this brought me. It is not strange then to see how, throughout my career, I was always seen as the 'dependable' cast member who could be relied upon to fill in for anyone at short notice and when asked to jump would always ask 'how high?' I was addicted to pleasing everyone and readily took on the mask of reliability in order to achieve this. For the first ten years of my career in professional theatre, I upheld my own personal record of never missing a show for illness, injury or for any other reason and it actually took the untimely death of my mother (when I was 29 and she was just 56) for me to not be in the theatre at the half-hour call. Even amidst the obvious tumult of emotions I experienced during this time, I still could not escape the nagging feelings of discomfort and anxiety at having broken that record. Add to that the fact that my mother had been a dancer herself, and had also passed on to me the professional mantra of 'the show must go on', I also felt that this is what she would have wanted. As it was, I only took one week off and then returned to work amidst more back-slapping and congratulations for apparently handling it all so well. Not surprisingly, my body knew otherwise and six months later it not only said but shouted *"No!"* This was my first inkling that the 'Cloak of Invincibility' which I had cultivated and worn with such pride for so long was not only an illusion, but a delusion. I was not at all the person I had convinced myself to be and my body was finally demanding that I wake up and accept that fact. I am not going to claim that my life radically changed in that moment and that I immediately saw the light, but over the subsequent years I have been on a journey of discovery which has led to me to question the very foundations on which I had based my sense of self, in order to reach a more authentic place. I have learned the very important art of saying 'no' (interesting that I should call this an art!) and endeavor to present my true self to those with whom I interact, rather than the version of me that I think will be best accepted. It is still a work in progress!

There is another aspect of the relationship to pain where the symptoms can actually be perceived to be useful to the performer to manage a particular situation. This is a phenomenon which I have encountered as a therapist, mostly amongst my dancer patients, but also to a lesser extent in other performers. It more commonly occurs in the situation of a long term injury which has removed the performer from his or her normal working routine. The initial injury will have likely caused much anxiety and the performer may have been in the uncomfortable position of having to cease training or disrupt a performance schedule. This would result in the performer being removed from his or her normal environment. As time goes on, and treatment progresses, a return to practice will usually be mooted and a schedule put in place for this. However, if the performer has been away from the working environment for a while, this is likely to result in a degree of deconditioning and an anxiety can start to build around returning to work. Questions begin to arise such as "What if I can't regain my fitness?", "What if I can no longer pull off that triple pirouette?", "What if my understudy was better than me?", "What if I can't get another job?" – the 'what ifs' start to take over and fear of failure abounds. The state of being injured can then start to become a relatively more comfortable place to be, providing a very convenient excuse for not being able to achieve all that is believed to be necessary. 'I didn't get that job because I still have this injury", "I can't pull off that triple pirouette because my foot isn't strong enough yet" – there is an excuse to fail. As a therapist, I have had several experiences of this situation where the level of pain expressed to me by the performer is no longer consistent with the level of tissue damage or injury that I am seeing. I may be very happy with the recovery of the injured area, but my patient is still reporting persistent symptoms. Again, I would not for one moment suggest that these symptoms are imagined, but perhaps there has been a transference of the anxiety surrounding the injury to the fear of no longer measuring up after an enforced absence, and we have already discussed the effect this anxiety may have on the amplification of pain levels. The key is for both the performer and the therapist to be clear on the exact source of the anxiety and pain and to ensure that the whole picture is addressed.

I have also seen instances of almost miraculous recovery of symptoms when an emotional stressor has been removed. Miracles are really just occurrences for which we have no explanation and in situations of spontaneous recovery it is usually the case that the true source of the symptoms has been misunderstood. I can give an example of this from a young student dancer whom I was treating for a muscle injury. When treating minors (those under the age of 16), I am required by law to have a parent or guardian present; in this case, it was the mother. I will be talking more about the parental role in performing arts training and, in particular, 'Ballet Mums' in the next chapter, but this is not an untypical example. The student in question had strained a muscle in her leg and this was failing to resolve naturally, so the mother brought her to me for treatment. I diagnosed a fairly straightforward muscle strain and began her on a course of manual therapy. It is my practice, when treating a minor, always to direct my questions to the child and ensure that my focus of attention is with the child at all times. However in this instance, the mother would always reply for the child and would talk over her at any time she tried to speak herself. The child was extremely 'moody' as a result, which often made the sessions uncomfortable for all. We agreed to modify her training initially to optimize her recovery but, after three sessions, I was happy enough with her progress to recommend a return to full activities. During the first session, the mother had mentioned to me that the child was due to audition for a leading vocational Ballet school in a few weeks' time, and there was some notable anxiety on the part of the mother as to whether she would be fit for this. When I asked the child if going to this school was a long-held dream for her (as is the case for many young dancers), she seemed less than enthusiastic about the idea, despite her mother's protestations that this was what she had always wanted. After returning to full activities the child continued to present for treatment insisting that her symptoms were unchanged, although I could find no physical evidence for this as the muscle appeared to me to be well healed. The audition date arrived and I said that I was happy for her to go ahead as long as she felt comfortable doing so. However, I also recognized that this was not necessarily a decision that the child would be allowed to make for herself. She returned to see me the week after the audition and, whilst she was getting changed for our session, her mother took me aside to tell me that she had sadly not passed the audition, and asked that I shouldn't mention anything about it as her daughter was devastated. At that moment the child came bounding into the room, grinning from ear to ear and saying that her leg now felt perfectly fine and she was really enjoying being back in full activities. There was no palpable difference to me in the condition of the muscle from the previous session, but what was clear was that the pressure of an audition for a school she really didn't want to attend, as it would have taken her away from her friends and social group, had been weighing very heavily on these young shoulders. Once released from this burden, the anxiety, and therefore pain, had resolved. The glum expression had now transferred to the mother and the roles had been reversed!

These are just some examples of the psyche manifesting in physical symptoms, either through anxiety or as a means to control one's situation or environment. This emphasizes the importance of taking a contextualized view of the whole picture when one is experiencing symptoms of pain, or dealing with those who are, and being able to correctly interpret the messages that the body is providing. Being absolutely honest with oneself about the origin of, and contributing factors to, the symptoms is the route to recovery – the authentic approach. Certainty is a dangerous illusion, particularly for health practitioners who must remain open to all possibilities. Iain McGilchrist writes:

> The only certainty, it seems to me, is that those who believe they are certainly right are certainly wrong.[9, p.460]

Selye also describes the biggest of all blocks to improvement as being "the certainty of being right".[1, p.16] Many of the greatest scientific and technological advances in history have been the result of chance, serendipity and intuition. We need to approach pain and injury with creative, open attention and engage in a reciprocal dialogue with it to ensure optimal results. After all, science is an art too and when medicine strives only for certainty and dismisses all other more implicit concepts then this can leave the performer feeling isolated and misunderstood, forming another block to recovery.

In the previous chapter, I made mention of the connection between creativity and some mood disorders. The constituents of a creative personality have been documented by neurologists and include such traits as being resourceful, open to new experiences, driven, ambitious, impulsive and sometimes hostile and asocial. This category also includes creative scientists as well as artists. However, a study by Feist in 1999 compared creative scientists and artists to each other, and the results found that artists were likely to be more anxious, emotionally labile, impulsive, asocial and show higher psychoticism than their scientific counterparts.[19] I previously mentioned the neurologist Stavia Blunt's statement that "the depressive experience is invaluable to the creative process"[14, p.43] but there are other neuropsychiatric conditions such as Bi Polar Disorder (BPD), Obsessive Compulsive Disorder (OCD) and Attention Deficit Hyperactivity Disorder (ADHD), which have also been associated with creativity.[14, p.44] Whilst there are genetic factors underlying most of these disorders, just because you may possess a gene for a particular condition in no way means that you will inevitably develop it. There has to be some sort of trigger for the process, which is usually environmental in origin, and stress is often at the top of the list. To quote Blunt once more:

> The creative brain is a neurodevelopmental phenomenon resulting from genetic and environmental interactions.[14, p.53]

Many artistic people will describe episodes when they experience a surge in their creative productivity, often accompanied by feelings of euphoria. However, these can also often be followed by periods of depression and creative blockage. Blunt has been investigating the theory that this is connected with dysregulation of some neurotransmitters (chemical messengers in the brain) such as Dopamine (DA) and that this dysregulation is a "fundamental property of the creative brain".[14, p.53] When DA transmission is too high then states of high energy, mania and psychosis may ensue. When it is too low, depression, social withdrawal and fatigue are experienced. This pendulum-like swing to the extremes of emotion again reflects the duality we explored in the previous chapter. Dopamine has also been linked with the processing of pain, so it may be another consideration contributing to our earlier exploration of pain perception in this population.

The list of famous performers who are known to have suffered from some sort of mental illness involving volatile mood swings is further evidence of this connection with creativity: Beethoven (BPD), Schumann (melancholic depression), Tchaikowsky (depression), Winona Ryder (depression), Kurt Cobain (ADHD, BPD), Carrie Fisher (BPD), Woody Allen (depression) are just some examples. Both Mozart and Michael Jackson are postulated to have suffered from an overlap of OCD and BPD with Tourette's Syndrome (TS) which is characterized by vocal and physical tics. Blunt sees the evidence of Jackson's potential TS in the vocal and physical tics characteristic of his singing and dancing style.[14, p.44] An interesting observation where what may be categorized as pathological symptoms can actually enhance the creative output.

Iain McGilchrist, in his work on cerebral lateralization (the tendency for right or left cerebral hemisphere dominance), proposes that there may also be a link between this concept and creativity. He adds that such lateralization may lead to both unusual talents and unusual deficits in the form of major mental illness. He continues by saying that nature would usually 'breed out' any genetic traits which may be detrimental to both an individual and the population at large and would only preserve them if they have some other important benefit.[9, p.13] He suggests that mental illness may be the price we pay for preserving the potential for creative talents – an argument he admits is contentious, but nonetheless, I think is worthy of consideration.

Following this train of thought, I previously mentioned the idea that the left hemisphere deals with joyful or positive emotions whilst the right hemisphere deals with sadness or emotions that are commonly deemed to be negative. The mistake here is to see sadness as a negative emotion which is somehow equated with being bad. McGilchrist states that:

> to be without the capacity for sadness would mean a degree of detachment from the manifestly suffering world around one which bordered on the psychopathic.[9, p.337]

When we start to label thoughts and emotions as 'positive' and 'negative', thereby categorising them as 'good' or 'bad', we can find ourselves on a rather slippery slope. If positive thinking is being used as a means to tune-out negative thoughts, this is actually a path to a state of delusion. Dr Gabor Maté calls this a "terminal optimism" and continues:

> As soon as we qualify the word *thinking* with the adjective *positive*, we exclude those parts of reality that strike us as "negative".[2, p.244]

He says that this so-called 'negative' thinking is actually the path to health, as it directs us to ask the awkward questions about what has led us to this point and what the body is trying to tell us. As Selye says, nature is quite indifferent to the concepts of good and bad, it can only say 'yes' or 'no', so we need to ask the right questions.[1, p.19] Once more we return to the concept of balance: we need to have a balanced view of the positive and negative emotions we are experiencing in order to have all the information necessary to make the right decisions about how we conduct ourselves in life. The people who are always 'up' and smilingly take on everything that is thrown at them, no matter what the personal cost (the person I was for many years!), are just as at risk of ill health as the people who cannot drag themselves out of bed because they feel their talents are unappreciated, and have lost themselves in a pit of despair. We are all outsourcing our personal value and worth to an external 'audience'.

So is pain a necessary or inevitable part of being a performer? Anything that places large demands on the musculoskeletal system is likely to induce pain and discomfort and, in the world of the elite performer, we are often pushing our body tissues to the limits of their tolerance. It could also be argued that without the experience of physical and emotional pain a performer would not be able to authentically express the underlying melancholy that is so fundamental to the arts and to human expression. You need to have an experiential reference in order to authentically reproduce an emotion or expression through music, movement or words. Historically, artists would shun material wealth, preferring to live in poverty and were often seen to live quite tortuous existences whilst producing great works which may not have been recognized as such at the time. However, I believe that while pain has its place, it is often taken to unnecessary extremes fuelled by the training culture of the performing arts. Pain is there as a message to be heard, understood and addressed, not to be ignored or heralded as a sign of achievement to be applauded by all. When dealing with a population that is arguably addicted to applause, such adulation should be meted out appropriately and with care, otherwise those wonderfully adaptable neurones and chemical messengers will be working away to ensure this behavior is reinforced to feed the addiction. Whilst performers undoubtedly hold the ultimate responsibility for managing their physiology, great care must be taken by parents and teachers in how our young performers' attitudes to pain are developed. We must not fall into the trap of fostering young artists who positively correlate pain with achievement as it is a very destructive path. This forms the subject of the next chapter.

Pain is a wonderful teacher and pain and injury can actually present an excellent opportunity to learn more about ourselves. When dealing with injured performers, I will always highlight to them how this can actually be a fortuitous event, allowing them to take a good look 'under the hood' of their body and gain some incredibly useful knowledge to ensure they are better protected in the future. Embracing the negative reactions that pain usually brings may prove a reality check for someone who has been in the habit of denying these signs, but releasing these delusions and accepting the realities of the body's limits of tolerance is the path to a more authentic, and therefore healthy, life. As performing artists we also have at our disposal one of the most potent curatives for all ills – the arts themselves. The seventeenth century scholar Robert Burton in his famous work, the rather appropriately named *Anatomy of Melancholy*, wrote of divine music that:

> Besides that excellent power it hath to expel many other diseases, it is a sovereign remedy against despair and melancholy.[20]

If we choose to listen, our bodies will give us the appropriate guiding signals whilst providing us with all the necessary pharmacological remedies we need to achieve health. Added to that, we then have the capacity to immerse ourselves in a nutritious pool of music, dance, poetry, prose and art, whose healing properties have been well documented for centuries – what more do we need?

4

A career in the arts: true destiny or meeting expectations?

Most artists would describe their career path as a calling rather than a conscious choice – the art chose them not the other way around. However, art in the modern world has become rather a different phenomenon – one can choose it as a career. In Chapter 2, we explored the origins of art as being a fundamental means of communication and expression, but now it has also become a means of earning money. People may be instinctively drawn to being a performing artist from an inherent need for artistic expression, but they may also end up relying upon it as a means of financial survival. The structure of modern civilization dictates that we must all have a job and earn a living in order to keep our place in society: whilst art may remain a source of escapism for some, for many performing artists themselves it has become a profession. For certain artists, this can prove to be a contradiction and may actually result in a negative relationship with the craft which they began by loving. When artistic achievement becomes entangled with the gaining of material wealth, we have a dichotomy that can have far reaching implications for the happiness and health of the performer. It will also necessarily give rise to an element of competition, putting us back on a linear, acquisitive ladder of progression so at odds with the circular, reciprocal nature of artistic expression – the art, once again, becomes a sport.

Maestro, operatic diva, virtuoso musician, prima ballerina, film star, pop star, these are all descriptive labels which evoke, for many, the idea of an aspirational, desirable goal to achieve in the performing arts. In the acquisitional culture of today's modern world the end goal of the societal status, which is perceived to come with such nomenclature, can all too often skew the flow of the natural journey to becoming accomplished in a particular discipline. We go back to the 'how fast can I get there' approach and focus on an endpoint of a seemingly linear journey. Even if the artists themselves set out with no particular end goal in mind, if they show a particular talent for their craft, this may bring them under pressure from those around them, who might feel it necessary to push them relentlessly along a treadmill towards some such gleaming celestial target. However, stars are beyond our grasp and, in my opinion, should remain so!

This brings us to the thorny issue of the roles of parents and teachers in the development of a budding performer. Whilst many parents may have a genuine desire to support their children's creative talents by facilitating their training without placing any undue pressure on their young shoulders, there are others who may become swept up in the perceived glamour of the life of a star performer and begin to drive their children towards this apparent goal. It is then that the boundaries between support and pressure become skewed and children may find themselves on a path driven by external expectations rather than by their own enjoyment. The somewhat pejorative terms such as 'helicopter parents', 'pushy parents', and 'ballet mums' will be familiar to many who are involved the world of the performing arts, as these people are, by their very nature, ever present. These types of parents may be driven by a desire for their child to achieve financial stability through notoriety, or may perhaps be vicariously living out an unfulfilled dream of their own, but the result is that the child becomes pushed in a forced linear direction, that ultimately only serves to stifle the creative process which, by its implicit nature, cannot be unidirectional. This over-vigilant type of parenting is usually based in love and concern, not in neglect, and is usually well-intentioned, if a little misguided, but the result becomes more an issue of the parent being over-present. According to the author Katie Roiphe in her article "The Seven Myths of Helicopter Parenting", this over-presence is the:

> wrong kind of presence. In fact it can reasonably be read by children as absence, as not caring about what is really going on with them.[21]

In this situation, the parents are more focused on what they want their child to become, rather than on who the child really is. She adds:

> if you are anxiously trying to make your child into a successful adult, you are most likely communicating anxiety—and not success—to them.

So here are the aforementioned themes of the emotional absence of the caregiver, and the transmission of anxiety from parent to child, which can lead to the blurred emotional and physiological boundaries discussed in the first chapter as being potentially harmful to our health.

These parents often devote huge amounts of their time (and money) to the training activities of their child, sometimes at the expense of other siblings, and this, in itself, can portray a very unhealthy message. Another writer on this subject is the psychologist Madeline Levine who, in her book *Teach Your Children Well: Parenting for Authentic Success*, asks of mothers:

> if you're willing to give up your own life and identity, what is the message you have sent your kid about the value of other people, mothers in particular?[22]

Parents who subjugate their own identity will not empower their children to develop their own strong sense of self esteem. If large financial sacrifices are also being made to support the child's training, this can represent a heavy burden of responsibility for the child to carry.

The result may be that the child develops a sense of having to achieve in order to not let others down, rather than achieving for his or her own personal fulfillment. If undue amounts of parental time and resources are being devoted to one child, resentment may begin to build in any siblings, leading to their feeling unduly neglected. For the apparently 'indulged' child, this can result in feeling further alienated from the family group. We have already seen the effects that low self esteem and a sense of isolation from the tribe can have on the physiological stress mechanism, so if this situation is present in the child's home, which should be his or her place of safety and refuge, is it any wonder we may begin to see some poor coping strategies being developed?

The competitive element will also be a factor here. The 'pushy parent' may seek external ratification of their child's success in the form of exam grades, trophies or leading roles in school productions, which inevitably invites comparison with fellow students. Competitions and auditions can become a routine part of the training process, placing the child in a series of anxiety-producing situations. Even the relative comfort of the classroom may become a battleground of comparison with one's peers. One thing I have noted in recent years, particularly in the dance world, is the growing number of extra-curricular activities available, such as youth performance groups, competitions and holiday courses, which are all supplementary to the students' core training programs. Although I was in full-time vocational training from a young age, our holiday times were not filled with endless courses and seminars – a holiday was a holiday. Today, it seems that students spend their school breaks on a rolling treadmill of courses which allow no time for either physical or mental respite. I have been on the faculty of one such summer school for classical dancers for many years: it is notable that whilst it used to be the case, in the early days, that ours would be the only course the participating students might choose to undertake during their summer break, today the students often arrive at the course having already attended two or three others, and are often going straight on to yet another course when ours is finished. There is almost a sense of panic that if students take any amount of time away from training, they will never 'make it'. There is also often a sense, particularly from talking to their parents, that children have to be 'seen' by the right people at these various courses, in order to assure their progression in this competitive field, and if they are absent, they may as well be invisible. What I have also noted over this same time period is the relative increase in injuries reported by the students. At the start of our summer course, students are asked to report any ongoing injuries to me so that I can ensure we manage them safely during the week. In earlier years, there would typically be only one or two students reporting injuries, whilst today that number has significantly increased to the stage where the students reporting injuries are almost in the majority. When I ask the injured students about their regular activity levels during term time and school holidays, there is often a notable lack of any rest or recovery time and any suggestions on my part, either to the student or parent, to make rest a priority are usually met with a look of horror! Whilst the resistance to taking rest time on the part of the student is something I can understand, and with which I can sympathize, the resistance from a parent, who cannot be persuaded that their child needs to take a break for his or her own health and safety, is something with which I struggle to come to terms. The notion that parents are helping their children by pushing them relentlessly towards a perceived goal of achievement within their art, regardless of the physical and emotional cost, is a dangerous path to take.

This sort of external pressure on the student performer may not only be being delivered by an over-anxious parent, but also by teachers, who play a vital role in the development of a young performer. In some cases, particularly where a child is undergoing intensive training, the teacher can almost assume the role of a parent or primary care-giver in terms of the amount of time spent with the student and the emotional attachment which may be formed. I have occasionally heard students say that they spend more time with their teacher than their parents or family and some, particularly amongst music students, have even gone to live with a teacher when intensive one-to-one training has been deemed necessary. There are some teachers who have been afforded very high status, either due to their own professional achievements or to the achievements of their students, and, in this situation, parents may often endow them with decision-making capacities for their child without question, thereby placing the teacher in a position of ultimate authority. The role of the teacher, therefore, is also absolutely critical to the emotional and physical wellbeing of the student and will be explored more thoroughly in the next chapter.

So the question is whether student performers are really on a path to fulfilling their true destiny, or whether they are merely meeting the expectations of those around them. Whilst they may have an innate talent that lends itself to an exceptional ability in a particular craft, when this comes under the grasp of an aspirational parent, or teacher, does their natural ability become choked by the external pressure to succeed? Let us return to the analogy of the right and left hemispheres of the brain: natural expression begins in the right hemisphere and is then passed to the left for the linear process of constructive training, but then needs to be returned to the right for creative expression and interpretation. If students are being forced into a relentless training program, without time for respite and recovery, and are also subject to the pressures of expectation from parents or teachers, are they in danger of remaining locked into left hemispherical, mechanistic patterns and losing the joy of creative expression? If they begin to feel that this career path is being forced upon them and that they are unable to escape, this lack of autonomy may eventually result in a physical manifestation of symptoms, as their body cries out for the expression of these repressed emotions. It may also lead to the situation where they are subjugating their own needs and desires to satisfy those of the people around them. Being responsible for someone else's disappointment is a huge burden to place on children – and one that is likely to have a profound effect on their developing physiology.

Once the joy and personal expression of their art has been lost, performers can begin to resent the very craft that began by being their passion. Most performers view their art not as a profession (i.e. 'what I do') but as an expression of themselves (i.e. 'who I am'). When we take into account how closely performers' identities are wrapped up in their art, anything which threatens this ability to express themselves through their creativity can have profound psychological (and therefore physiological) implications. Without the ability to escape into their art form, the world becomes an unhappier place. The high number of cases of depressive illness amongst performers, explored in Chapter 3, highlights the fine line they often tread between the joy of expression and the darkness of a world without it.

Another issue that can result in a loss of the joy of creative expression arises when performers need to earn a living from their craft. When the performance becomes a means of financial survival, the boundaries begin to blur both emotionally and physiologically. Most performers, whatever their discipline, will usually have a leaning towards a particular style or repertoire with which they resonate. A dancer may prefer classical ballet, jazz, folk, tap, etc., and within those styles, may particularly favor a specific choreographer (Balanchine, MacMillan, Fosse, etc.). Similarly, a musician may favor classical, rock, jazz, or metal and may specialize in a particular composer's work, or may prefer only to perform his or her own compositions. Likewise, actors may prefer performing Shakespeare, or Alan Bennett's works, or may form partnerships with specific film or theatre directors. However, the opportunities to perform these particular works may well be few and far between, and prove limiting. When one is trying to earn a living from one's art form, sticking to these ideals may well lead to financial hardship and an inability to perform one's craft at all. Therefore, performers are forced to take whatever work comes their way, even if it is performing repertoire which they find to be soul destroying. A bass player whose passion lies in avant garde jazz, but is unable to find an audience or outlet for this, may find himself taking work with a 70's Disco tribute band in order to pay the bills, and feels a little piece of himself die every time he plays "I Will Survive" for the umpteenth time! This sense of dejection can chip away at one's spirit and lead to a very negative relationship with the profession. In my experience of treating performers, it can also be an underlying factor in the development of musculoskeletal pain, mediated via the stress mechanisms previously explored, and can also have a negative impact on their capacity to heal. In this situation, performers are being distanced from their authentic selves and therefore disconnected from their bodies. (I should just note for the record that I personally have nothing against 70's music and for another musician, this may well be their passion!).

The life of a touring performer can also raise difficult issues, particularly with respect to family relationships. If performers are reliant upon their craft for providing an income for their family and the only job available at a given time is a nine month tour, this can raise a dilemma. If in order to provide for your family you need to be taken away from them, it can be a very difficult position in which to find yourself. If you add into the equation a tour that might be of a show that you hate, and will therefore not even provide you with emotional or professional fulfillment, then it can be a soul destroying experience. Even if the tour is professionally rewarding, the separation from loved ones may create an emotional stressor which may lead to ill health. Some touring performers may have resigned themselves to a life without a long term partner or children, as their lifestyle was not conducive to maintaining a stable relationship. This can sometimes be balanced by the formation of a family-like structure with your fellow performers. But there can also be times when you are stuck with a touring group with whom you have no emotional connection and even, potentially, dislike. With the high pressures involved in performance and the demonstrative (and sometimes volatile) nature of some creative artists, this may result in some explosive interactions, leading to further social and emotional isolation. I have come across many performers who, particularly after having reached a certain age, have made the decision not to take any more touring work, and who would rather find a 'day job' completely unrelated to the performing arts, in order to supplement their income whilst waiting for that dream job closer to home. Others may feel very comfortable with the gipsy life, but if they are forced to retire, either through injury or age, they may find themselves completely lost and without direction. One such touring musician, who is of advancing years, has told me categorically that when the time comes that he can no longer play, he will simply 'take a pill' rather than face a life without performing. This may be an extreme case, but we must be aware of the extent to which performers can become identified with their art and take pains to ensure that they have a support structure for transitioning out of their art, should this become necessary. Training should prepare them for this eventuality, and mechanisms for de-training should be in place. These will be discussed in subsequent chapters.

What this all boils down to is whether the reality of what it is to be a performer in the modern world actually meets the expectations of the young aspiring artist. Whilst students may have dreamed of what that life would be like when they, for example, joined that famous ballet company, the reality may be something quite different. Young ballet dancers, for example, will have trained for many years and achieved the skills to perform incredibly complex and intricate movements. During their training, they will have learned and possibly performed some of the main roles in the classical ballet repertoire, and be able to execute steps requiring high levels of virtuosity. Once they have been selected to join a ballet company (a great achievement in its own right), the ladder of progression doesn't stop there. There may be another six or seven rungs of that ladder to be climbed before one reaches the ranks of a principal dancer, and potentially one of international repute. The reality for many dancers is that they will not progress that far in the rankings and may stay at the corps de ballet level, never having the opportunity to perform the solo roles for which they trained so hard. There will be many dancers who are very happy to be within the structure of the corps de ballet and do not wish to have the added pressure that promotion can bring, but others may find themselves unfulfilled by the lack of potential to really show their skills, leaving them feeling creatively stifled.

However, promotion too can bring unhappiness, particularly with regard to social relationships. I mentioned earlier the concept of a dancer who finds herself plucked from the general ranks of a company, to be promoted, first to a soloist, then a principal dancer. Recalling how dance originated as an embodiment of music which served to promote bonding within a group, it is, by its nature, a group activity. During a classical dancer's training and subsequently in the corps de ballet of a company, one is very much part of a professional and social group. The hours of training and the professional workload (being in the theatre from 9.30 am to 10.30 pm, six days a week) often dictate that there is little time for being an active part of an external social group. As a result, your fellow dancers become both your family and friends, as well as colleagues. You will share dressing rooms (and some may even share home accommodation), and your rehearsal and performance schedules will usually be roughly the same. Once dancers begin to progress up the ranks, they are likely to become further removed from the group structure, as the roles they are dancing will often require one-to-one rehearsal. Principal dancers will also usually be given their own dressing room, away from their peers. Whilst a private room with a star on the door is something to which many young performers may aspire, the reality can be quite isolating. The gossip and chat of the communal dressing room, and the comfort of having your friends around you is something often missed by those dancers who have progressed up the rankings. The competitive nature of the performance world may also lead to a build-up of resentment to your success amongst some of your peer group, further deepening the sense of isolation. Now, also, you have the added pressure of living up to the expectations of holding that position within the company. The old saying of 'when you're at the top, the only way is down' may leave you feeling particularly vulnerable. Not only will there be pressures to perform from within the company (management, choreographers, artistic directors etc.), but you now also have the added expectations of the audience and the ever-present media critics. If one or two members of the corps de ballet don't perform well, then it will often be the whole corps that is criticized, but if you are in the leading role and have an off-day, then there is only one place to lay the blame. You are exposed and vulnerable, and perhaps lacking a support group, which is a very uncomfortable place to be. It takes a very strong sense of self and autonomy to be able to deal with such pressures and certainly won't be within everyone's capabilities to handle. For some, this perceived ideal goal of being a leading dancer, with the roles and lifestyle that go with it, is not quite all that it was cracked up to be. This phenomenon is not limited to the ballet world; I have seen several people in this position, from all branches of the arts who, as a result of these pressures, have manifested symptoms of pain or illness from which they found it difficult to recover. I mentioned in the previous chapter the issue of an injury becoming a convenient excuse for not performing, and I have seen several cases of persistent symptoms in those at the top of their profession, where perhaps the pressures had become intolerable and, for as long as they remain in the line of fire, the body will continue its protest.

It may be the case that for performers who have reached the top of their profession, the motivation to pursue their craft is now more related to the meeting of external expectations and commitments, rather than emanating from the pure joy of their art form. The audience, critics, media, directors and fellow performers collectively form a 'house of cards' which may come tumbling down if you don't turn up to do your job. The phrase 'I will let everyone down' is one I have heard many times from performers when a suggestion has been made to take some time out. This reflects the subjugation of one's own needs for physical recovery, for the sake of sparing other people some difficulties. Such behavior, we have seen, can be the precursor to illness. The precariousness of their position in the profession also represents a potent fear for such performers – if they miss one performance, they may be resigned to the professional scrapheap. A high pedestal is no place for an acrophobic, so they may live their time in this position in a state of constant anxiety and, therefore, be subject to the physiologic responses that we have seen may result.

If the fulfillment of your goal leads to a sense of emptiness and isolation, what does this say about your authenticity? Have you in fact been living out someone else's dream or perhaps become so swept up in the momentum surrounding your training and professional achievements, that your career has actually become more of a habit than a true choice? One particular high-ranking performer, for whom I was providing treatment, would spend every session talking about her passion for interior design – she would absolutely light up when talking about it. But when the subject returned to her next performance, the light was rapidly extinguished and a sense of distance would creep into our discussions. I felt strongly that her authentic self no longer resided in her current career, but she was so firmly stuck in the habit and perceived security of that world that she would rapidly dismiss any attempts on my part to suggest a change.

Another phenomenon that is common amongst performers, and one which I have personally experienced (and still occasionally do!), is the sense of 'feeling a fraud' – that somehow, someone is going to catch you out as pretending to be someone you're not. This is something that I have heard from many performers and has also been echoed by several of the artists who have made contributions to this text. My father, a very successful TV director who is held in very high regard by all his peers, recently admitted to having also experienced this same sensation: when he was reading an early draft of this book and came across this subject, he recalls thinking "She's writing about me!" I had no idea that he had ever been anything less than fully confident in his abilities, as he always seemed to be in complete control in the TV studio, managing the cast, crew and the complexities of the technical components with such seeming ease and affability. However, he has now admitted that he often felt like he was 'making it up as he went along' and that someone soon might catch him out! This is actually a known psychological phenomenon called 'Impostor Syndrome' which was first written about by two psychologists, Pauline Clance and Suzanne Imes, in a 1978 article entitled "The impostor phenomenon in high achieving women: Dynamics and therapeutic intervention."[23] This sense of feeling a fraud is often experienced by successful or talented people and begins in childhood when the child is measuring his or her success by purely external means: an exam grade, a trophy, etc. Success, just as health, needs to be developed internally and the child needs to be the validator of his or her own achievements and not just rely on external praise or rewards. Madeline Levine says of this subject:

> Success that is not authentic, that doesn't feel real or 'owned,' never feels like success at all . . . . The 'impostor syndrome' that all of us feel from time to time becomes a permanent state of affairs for our children when success feels inauthentic.[23, p.xxv]

This all boils down to the aforementioned issue of building the appropriate self-esteem to ensure that children are following their true path, driven only by their own personal desire to express, rather than just meeting the external expectations of those around them. The route to promoting self esteem, and the issues of developing talent will be explored more fully in the next chapter.

We live in a society that continues to value competitive, hierarchical structures and the performing arts have come to reflect this. The higher you move up the ladder of achievement in the arts, the more exposed you become to the criticism and expectations of those around you. Art becomes relegated to a display of skills to an audience, rather than the collaborative medium which formed its evolutionary roots, and the artist, therefore, requires a very strong, grounded, authentic sense of self to weather the storm of attention without suffering any detrimental effects. So does the way we train and nurture our young performers for a life in the arts really prepare them for the reality of the profession as it stands today? And does that help them to manage the issues we have explored here? This forms the subject of the next chapter.

5

Perseverance or abuse?
The balance of training

There is an often-cited notion which says that it takes some 10,000 hours of training to become an expert in a particular skill. This was first popularized in 2008 by the journalist and author Malcolm Gladwell in his book *Outliers*[24] and was based on research by K. Anders Ericsson *et al*[25] into the playing habits of elite violinists and an earlier paper by Herbert Simon and William Chase on skilled chess players.[25] Although there are those who contest this idea, and child prodigies would be a notable exception to the rule, it is fair to say that to become a skilled performer you will need to spend a large amount of your life in training. In the case of most professional musicians and dancers, this training will start early in childhood. We have already discussed the importance of the relationship of children with their caregivers and with their social environment in developing both their emotional and physical wellbeing. So how well is this supported by the world of performing arts training?

My own personal experience of intense training is echoed both by the anecdotal evidence of my performing arts colleagues, and by my performer patients. The picture painted is one of a culture of fear-based instruction, underpinned by negative reinforcement, with the teacher-student relationship being very much a dictatorship, rather than a democracy. Whilst I know of many wonderful teachers who do much to empower their students and promote their self confidence (and I have had several teachers along the way who did this for me), it cannot be denied that, historically, the general trend in performing arts training has always been towards engendering the 'survival of the fittest' notion, where only those who can tolerate assaults on both physical and emotional levels have any hope of weathering the storm of a performing arts career, and the way to prepare them for this is through an education in the 'school of hard knocks'. Although there is growing recognition that this may not be the best approach to develop young, healthy performers, it is still being talked about as a current issue at every performing arts medicine conference I attend, in every part of the world. However far we think we have come from the images of the old Russian Ballet Master or Mistress wielding a stick at their students, or string players being forced to play until their fingers bleed, unfortunately many such experiences have been handed down through generations of teachers. This, then serves to perpetuate the myth that unless you can put up with a constant undermining of your confidence, and high levels of pain, you will never 'make it'. This notion is also reinforced by popular culture and I am reminded of the opening credits of the US TV series of *Fame* where each week, the dance teacher, played by Debbie Allen, was heard saying to a class of dancers:

> You've got big dreams? You want fame? Well, fame costs. And
> right here is where you start paying . . . in sweat.

Although the words 'blood and tears' were not included, I think they were certainly implied! If memory serves, I believe she was also banging the obligatory stick on the floor at the time for added emphasis. These sorts of images help to perpetuate the notion that being yelled at, belittled and disparaged, whilst pushing your body through the pain to the limits of its tolerance, is the best way to produce a performer or to nurture talent.

If we return to the concepts of health explored in the earlier chapters we can see where this sort of negative training behavior may lead.

When we consider the sensitive nature of most creative individuals, is it any wonder that many of our artists develop perfectionist tendencies, obsessive behaviors, and live with a constant fear of failure if they have spent their childhood in such fear-based environments? Is this a necessary part of creating an elite performer, or have we become snagged by a cultural myth enmeshed in the modern world's tendency towards competitive, acquisitional goal seeking? The message in the current literature from the world of performance psychology is that fear-based training is most certainly not the way to create elite professionals.

Clearly, in order to pursue a career in the performing arts, one must have high levels of motivation to weather the inevitable ups and downs of this often volatile profession. But when does motivation become an obsession, and how does this relate to the perfectionist tendencies so often a trait of the performing artist? Motivation is multi-faceted: it can be driven by the joy of a wonderfully creative experience that we wish to repeat and this is known as intrinsic motivation. However, it can equally be driven by fear: "I have to keep trying or I will be a complete failure"; "If I don't hit that top B flat, the musical director will yell at me". This is extrinsic motivation driven by an external reward or punishment. So when people say that you 'have to be motivated' to pursue a career in the arts, what do they really mean? When teachers say they are 'motivating' their students, are they just scaring them into achieving? Are they providing a positive or negative inducement? When dance teachers incentivize their students to master a triple pirouette by threatening to remove them from the school production if they fail, they might believe that this is providing motivation, but what they are actually doing is just inducing anxiety and further chipping away at the students' sense of self worth. That triple pirouette is now likely to be positively correlated with a fear response in their students and fear has no place in aiding you to balance on one leg and spin round three times with confidence!

Perfectionism is also multi-dimensional and doesn't necessarily have to be negative or destructive. A study into perfectionism in musicians by Stoeber and Eismann in 2007, states recent findings have shown that:

> ... only some facets of perfectionism are associated with anxiety and distress, whereas other facets are associated with positive characteristics and outcomes such as motivation and achievement.[27]

They showed that striving for perfection is associated with both higher effort and achievement and that this is a positive characteristic driven by autonomous reasons (intrinsic motivation). However, sometimes what the musicians actually reported was something more akin to a negative reaction to imperfection, rather than being positively driven, and this was found to be:

> ... associated with performance anxiety, emotional fatigue, and somatic symptoms, corroborating findings from previous studies that showed perfectionism to be a personality characteristic related to anxiety and distress in musicians.[27]

This negative reaction to imperfection is driven by extrinsic motivation and a feeling of being controlled by others. So this brings us back to the argument that striving for high standards of technical and artistic proficiency should not require that the student be exposed to extrinsic, negative forms of motivation from those around them, such as parents and teachers. If, however, students are supported in developing a strong sense of autonomy and confidence, they will be motivated to achieve by their own intrinsic drive for the joy of their craft, without the destructive effects of anxiety and fear.

Another negative aspect of perfectionism occurs when children develop a sense of self-worth that is contingent upon receiving positive feedback from parents and teachers regarding their abilities. Gifted children may be so used to being rewarded for their talents that they begin to perceive their whole sense of self worth as being contingent upon their level of achievement: this may lead to a sense of helplessness when they find themselves unable to meet those expectations. This is a fragile state in which to live, as any obstacles to achievement will be seen as a threat rather than a challenge and will be associated with a strong fear of failure. Another model of perfectionism, proposed by Flett *et al* in 2002. is the 'social reaction model', where a child may develop a need to appear perfect in order to be included in a social group. This links with the concepts explored in earlier chapters regarding our inherent need for social bonding for both our own personal health and the survival of the species as a whole. It is postulated that children in this category are likely to have been:

> exposed to a harsh environment of parental hostility and lack of warmth that may involve physical or psychological maltreatment including exposure to shame, excessive criticism and punishment.[28]

As we look at some of the training methods that have been the experience of many performing artists, I believe we will start to see links to the types of coping strategies that many of these artists come to develop and perhaps some explanations for the type of behaviors typical in this population.

Training pathways differ for the varied disciplines of the performing arts, but we will focus here on the typical experiences of aspiring musicians and dancers. In the case of instrumental musicians, initial experiences may be in the form of group music lessons, perhaps at their regular school, but once proficiency is noted, or a parent decides to place the child on a more structured training path, tutoring will usually be in the form of one-to-one contact with a teacher. In contrast, most dance training will be done in the group setting of a class, where several students are trained simultaneously (although occasionally private tuition will also be sought). Some students may attend a full-time vocational school from as young as seven or eight years old, where their arts training is provided in conjunction with their academic schooling, and these may be either day or boarding schools. Others may remain at their regular school and pursue their arts training in extra-curricular programs. The common themes in all of these pathways are reflected in the number of contact hours the students will have with their teachers, the level of absorption they experience within their given art form and the affect this can have of skewing the balance of their lives. There are many standard models which are used to describe the optimal balance of life for health: these are often depicted as wheels or pie charts divided up into different colored categories for work, family, friends / relationships, recreation, physical activity, personal growth and community. An optimally balanced life would be shown by an equal slice of the pie for each of these categories. However, student performers may place their art form into many, if not all, of these categories such as work, recreation (when their art is also their hobby), friends / relationships (if they only ever interact with other performers), physical activity, personal growth and community (particularly if they attend a full-time vocational school) and, if they also come from a family of performers, perhaps the family bracket as well. The wheel then becomes predominantly one color and, clearly, there is little balance. When students' absorption in their chosen career path leads them to become blinkered to the multi-colored rainbow of life in the world around them, then should an injury or some other issue threaten to prevent them from pursuing a life in that career, this can be a frightening experience. When the art has become their whole identity, without it they neither know who they are, nor what they should do. This can be a precarious way to live.

Let us first take a look at the culture of music education, particularly in the classical field. As mentioned above, this will usually take place in a one-to-one setting with the teacher and, due to the high number of hours typically spent training, places that teacher in a highly responsible position in terms of both the professional and emotional development of the child. In the previous chapter, I commented that I have heard several musicians say that they probably spent more time with their teacher than with their own parents during their childhood. In addition, parents can often transfer much of the responsibility for their child's development to the teachers, allowing them final say on crucial decisions for the child's welfare. There are those teachers who do not allow parents to be present during training and, therefore, the parent may be completely unaware of what goes on in the lessons. They may be basing their choice of teacher on professional reputation and observable results, whilst being wholly unaware of the processes and methods being used to educate their child. Blind faith may seem quite rational when dealing with a maestro of international repute!

This 'closed system' approach to teaching is something I have also encountered through my therapeutic work with student performers. If I feel the injury or symptom, for which the student has presented to my clinic, is connected with a certain facet of his or her posture or technique (which is often the case), I will make recommendations for adjustments to these in order to relieve the load on the symptomatic area. On occasion, when making such suggestions, the response from the student has been 'but my teacher won't let me do that'. If I then ask whether the student could perhaps open a discussion with their teacher about how they might reach a compromise, in order to allow the injured area to heal, I am sometimes met with a look of horror, suggesting that any attempts to open a dialogue on these lines will land the student straight in the dog house. If I ask whether the student would like me to open a discussion with the teacher on their behalf, again the response is sometimes one of fear. Confidentiality is at the heart of every session with my patients, so if they don't want me to talk to their teacher, then I won't do it – at least in my clinic room they have will the autonomy to make their own decisions, whether based in fear or not! This just serves to underline the sad fact that many teaching situations are dictatorships, not democracies, which can only serve to blur those delicate developing emotional boundaries so vital to the student's current and future health. How one can hope to create freely expressive, authentically reciprocal music in these circumstances is a question some teachers should perhaps be asking themselves.

Time and again I hear stories of music students who are being trained in an environment of negative reinforcement. Rather than being encouraged and rewarded for achievement, they are punished for their mistakes. This does nothing to promote the students' self esteem and does not allow them to develop any autonomy in their art form.

When students are so immersed in their training that they rarely have a life outside their music, this harsh criticism becomes an assault not just on their ability to play, but on their whole identity. Students will inevitably begin to correlate their musical ability with their own sense of value, so any criticism is seen as an attack on their whole person and may lead to a situation of the contingent self-worth mentioned earlier. When your whole identity is wrapped up in your playing, when there are no other colors on your wheel of life, a crushing fear of failure is likely to be the result. Students may develop a predisposition to feeling that if their musical ability is not of a high enough standard, this means that they are also a complete failure as a person – their entire value structure is tied to their musical ability. This is something that is endemic in Western culture: that we are all judged by our perceived usefulness to society. One of the first things you are likely to be asked when meeting someone new is "So, what do you do?" Armed with this information, that person will be able to label you and find you an appropriate spot in the left-brained structured hierarchy with which things are generally measured in today's world. If, however, you feel you have no clear label with which to describe yourself, or if your answer to the question was 'nothing', then you are likely to placed in a category marked 'treat with suspicion' and given little or no value as a person. Students who are unable to play through injury, or think themselves unworthy of the title of 'musician' through lack of perceived ability, may just place themselves in that 'suspicion' bin without anyone else having to do it for them. Without being given the appropriate support to develop a balanced sense of self and autonomy through the guidance of a teacher or parent, the student is left vulnerable both emotionally and physiologically. Inevitably, the students I encounter are usually the ones suffering from pain, so the sample to which I am referring is probably biased. However, if we bear in mind the mechanisms previously explored connecting stress and anxiety to increased pain levels, then perhaps it is not surprising that it is the students presenting to me with pain who are reporting this sort of training behavior. I know for a fact that there are some wonderfully empowering music teachers out there, but I am probably less likely to see their students in my clinic, which says something in itself!

Whilst music students may spend many hours of training with their teacher, they will also be spending many hours practicing alone – I have treated many students and professionals who admit to anything up to nine hours of practice a day – sometimes more. Again, it has often been drilled into them that any less devotion than this to practice will mean that they will not progress to the top. The emphasis is often on quantity rather than quality of practice, leading to a notion that those requisite 10,000 hours all need to be done this week! On top of the physical toll that this will inevitably take on the body, it can also lead to a sense of isolation for young students, who will necessarily be giving up leisure time and social activities in devotion to their art. Research has shown that loneliness is linked with reduced immunity, via the emotional and physiological mechanisms which we have already explored, and once again we see the implicit social bonding nature of music being lost to a world of isolation. The closest some of these students may come to social contact with other children their age may be through competitions or orchestral practice with other young musicians. However both of these situations are likely to induce further anxiety as they now will have to bear the weight of comparison with others. If you are used to working in isolation, and particularly if your training has served to quash your sense of self esteem and autonomy, then the fear of failure will loom large and any interactions with your peers may serve to raise your stress levels. Some students won't even need the comparison with others to induce a stress response, the negative conditioning mentioned above will be enough for them to experience that fear of failure in the solitude of their own practice room. Dr Gabor Maté states that both acute and chronic stress experienced in childhood can lead to:

> an environmentally conditioned helplessness that permits neither
> of the normal responses of fight or flight.[2, p.20]

The ability to respond appropriately to stressful situations is lost and can lead to the repression of emotion discussed in earlier chapters:

this then leaves our physiological defense systems vulnerable to attack. When this behavior is so conditioned, students may not be able to recognize the threat that their environment poses and therefore make no attempts to remove themselves from it – just like the frog, they stay sitting in that pot of slowly boiling water.

The physical toll of hours of repetitive practice is also a huge issue. We have previously discussed the body's need for variety and how repetitive loading of local structures can lead to tissue damage and injury. Dr Hans Selye gives us a lovely analogy:

> The human body – like the tires on a car, or the rug on a floor – wears longest where it wears evenly.[1, p.433]

However, like so many aspects of the modern Western world, the physical requirements of music have been pushed to ever more extreme limits. Over history, musical instruments themselves have become more and more complex and, in the period from the seventeenth century onwards, we have seen great advances in their technical complexity, often driven by the composers of the day demanding greater tonal range. The original Fortepiano from around 1700 had just four octaves (an octave being comprised of eight notes): Mozart began to compose for five octaves, Beethoven increased this to six and by the nineteenth century, Liszt was composing for the 7.5 octave instruments we see today. Similar advances also occurred in other instruments, requiring musicians to have ever more refined sensorimotor skills, which in turn demand ever increasing hours of practice to develop. Dr Eckhart Altenmuller, a world-leading neurologist in the field of the neurophysiology and neuropsychology of musicians, suggests that we may perhaps have reached an evolutionary end point of the limits of manual dexterity in musicians. As an example of this, he points to musicians' dystonia, which is a rare condition of disordered brain mapping, occurring primarily in high level elite musicians, that results in aberrant muscle movements which can be career-ending. The human body can simply go no further. He also suggests that the advent of recorded music has driven musicians to achieve ever higher (and potentially unobtainable) goals by comparing live performance to studio recordings where there is:

> the possibility of obtaining and splicing multiple takes [which] contribute to an illusionary perfection as standard.[14, p.106]

Such recordings often feature world-class players, whose performances in the pre-digital era may only have been heard by a select few at their live concerts, but are now widely available for all to hear in the comfort of their living room. This presents a benchmark of achievement which serves to push young musicians to practice to ever greater lengths. I have the great privilege to be currently working with a world-renowned concert pianist, who was regaling me with stories of the hours recently spent sitting hunched over a mixing desk in a recording studio, wearing headphones and picking apart every detail of the latest recording and making adjustments. Whilst this, in itself, also represents yet another physical stress for the body of a musician, it may also lend credence to Altenmuller's thoughts that a 'live recording' may not be as authentic as it is perhaps represented to be.

Moving to the world of dance training, for students under the age of 16 this usually either takes place in a full time vocational institution (day or boarding) or as an extra-curricular activity whilst attending a regular academic school. However, from the age of 16 onwards, most students will be attending full time vocational training establishments and it is rare (though not impossible) for anyone to enter the dance profession without having done so. When auditioning for professional work, having a pre-professional school of high repute on your résumé is often a prerequisite for even being offered an audition, so competition for a place in such schools is high. All full time schools, whether from age 7 or 16, will require an entrance audition which means that students are conditioned early to this competitive element of the dance world. Even in local dance schools, regular examinations, as well as regional and national competitions, are often a major part of the training process, placing high burdens of expectation on young shoulders. As in music, the training hours demanded will be very high. Students on a pre-professional track, undertaking training on an extra-curricular basis at a local dance school, will often be doing up to three hours of dance every weekday evening, and sometimes all day on a Saturday, in addition to their regular academic schooling. At a full time vocational school, the day will often be divided in two with half spent on academic studies and the other half on vocational studies. I myself attended one such full-time school from the age of seven – it was a boarding school, however I attended as a day pupil as my family lived in the local town. On a typical day, I would arrive at school for 8.15 am assembly, and spend the morning in academic studies. After lunch we would don our leotards and spend three hours in either dance, drama or music training, until tea at 4.30 pm. From 5 pm, you would either be in supervised 'prep' classes to do your homework, in a rehearsal if there was an upcoming production, or in an extra dance class for a forthcoming exam. After supper, there would be 'second prep' for students over the age of twelve, for more homework. I would typically be collected by my parents at 8.30 pm having spent a whole twelve hours at school. I continued this pattern every day for nine years. We would often also have extra classes or rehearsals on a Saturday, although Sundays were, thankfully, a rest day! The school itself operated some very strict rules – although I was in attendance during the latter part of the 20th century, you may have been forgiven for thinking it was the Victorian age. On top of having to curtsey whenever you encountered a member of staff or a visitor, there were fingernail checks, hair checks, locker checks, 'knicker' checks (to ensure you had the regulation two pairs of underwear – yes two, one for under leotards, and another pair on top for regular wear), dorm inspections, and changing room inspections – all carrying fines for contravention of the rules. You could also be punished for wearing the wrong colored hair band (or not wearing one at all), wearing outdoor shoes when indoors and vice versa, wearing dance shoes anywhere other than in a dance studio, not wearing your cloak between lessons, being in the wrong room or the wrong corridor at the wrong time, using staircases or corridors which were 'out of bounds', not having nametags in your clothes, losing your property, speaking whilst standing in a queue for assembly or meals, speaking during 'prep' sessions, not wearing your school hat and gloves when off the premises (on the rare occasions you were allowed out) and heaven help you if you were caught with any kind of contraband food items, such as sweets! One lived in a constant state of fear that one of the surly matrons was lurking around the next corner, just waiting to catch you in a banned corridor at the wrong time of day in your tap shoes with your socks rolled down! Such conventions, I know, are not confined to performing arts schools – the issue of fear-based perfectionism is apparent in many walks of life and these stories may also ring true for many non-performers.

In terms of the schooling itself, there would be the usual academic exams, plus dance exams in many styles (ballet, modern, tap and national), music exams (with some students playing multiple instruments with exams for each), drama exams, annual in-school assessments, a dance show, drama show and a big annual school production. On top of this, there were often auditions for child roles in external professional productions, such as the one I mentioned before with London Festival Ballet. For the older students, there were also other in-house competitions such as the Ballet Cup, the Stage Cup, the Music Cup and the Drama Cup where you were pitted against your peers in solo performances. There was also the school Chamber Choir, for which an audition was required for a coveted place, and which was itself involved in the annual UK national 'Sainsbury's Choir of the Year' competition. So life was really one long battle to prove yourself and to keep your place in the ranks. All of these events were deemed to be preparing you for the competitive world of the professional theatre: that by somehow saturating you in endless competitions you would be better acclimatized to the inevitable stress that these situations induce. But does endless competition really breed a good competitor? In my own case, I would say most certainly not.

Throughout my childhood, I found exams and auditions to be very traumatic experiences in which I never felt I was able to do my best. Still to this day, I have an absolute horror of any kind of exam or competitive situation and, when faced with such situations, find myself fighting the urge to run screaming in the opposite direction! Yes, the world of professional theatre is a harsh and very competitive one, but would building a young students' sense of self esteem and autonomy not be a better way of preparing them for a life of competitive situations, rather than producing someone who is constantly choked by their own fear of failure? Dr Hans Selye, when discussing the stress of a job in the corporate world, talks of the 'Peter Principle' where:

> It is common practice to keep promoting personnel from jobs in which they performed competently to higher positions until they have reached a level at which they are incompetent.[1, p.373]

I think this is also true of dance training where, rather than being rewarded for incremental achievements, you are constantly pushed until you can go no further, at which point you are deemed a failure. The target is always moving further away, which leads to a sense that you will never be good enough. The Canadian prima ballerina Karen Kain, who had arguably reached the peak of her profession, is quoted as saying that out of some 10,000 performances in her professional career, she was only satisfied with about seven or eight of them.[29] Whilst those from outside the performing arts world may be shocked by this declaration, I can guarantee that many of the performers reading this text will be nodding their heads in recognition of that feeling. Despite high achievements, many performers never feel that they are good enough, which usually bears no relation to their level of skill – they simply don't have the necessary self esteem to recognize their abilities.

In the dance studio itself, particularly in a classical ballet setting, it is sometimes the case (although thankfully not as widespread as it once was) for students to have little or no voice in respect of their training. It is very much a 'don't speak unless spoken to' environment and then just answer, 'yes' or 'no'. Physical abuse, in its most obvious sense of corporal punishment, was thankfully not something I experienced personally, nor have I commonly heard it reported by those students whom I treat. Nevertheless, there are some rather heavy-handed techniques, which are seen by some as a traditional and necessary part of the training process, which may not be that far removed from the issue of bodily harm. I personally experienced some very aggressive stretching techniques aimed at improving flexibility. Some examples were being forcibly pushed down and held into the splits and having the teacher or another student push on your shoulders or stand on your hips for added emphasis. Another would be lying on your front and being pulled up by your arms into a backbend, perhaps with a helpful foot in your lower back for good measure! These kind of practices were actively encouraged and seemed quite natural (albeit painful) to us at the time. We were all too eager to 'help out' our friends with their stretching routines by way of a shove with a booted foot, as long as the offer was reciprocated! It was only when I began training in anatomy many years later that I would look back at these practices with watering eyes, wondering how it is that I can actually still walk! The sad fact is that teaching practices have been handed down for decades and decades, under the banner of 'if it worked for me, it will work for you'. And whilst anatomical and medical understanding grew apace in the outside world, the closeted world of dance training remained seemingly unaware of the damage that may be caused by such practices. Ballet, in particular, has changed hugely since the early 20th century when dancers' legs were rarely seen to pass beyond the level of their hips. However, as the demand for ever more gymnastic-like flexibility increased, training practices just became more heavy-handed to push the body further and further, without stopping to wonder whether this was still the best approach. Sadly, I am still hearing stories from young students of, for example, being forced to stand with their feet at 180 degrees of turn-out when they lack the strength to control their joints in this position and it is causing them injury. Again, as with the music students, if I ask whether they might be able to discuss the possibility of modifying this foot position with their teacher, at least whilst the injury heals and they build the necessary strength, many students will still shake their heads in muted terror at the thought of broaching this subject and are no more keen for me to do the talking either. There are changes being made in this regard, with anatomy and injury awareness now being part of the syllabus in most dance teacher training programs, however dance teaching is not a regulated profession and there are many teachers out there who are not attached to any teaching board. It is among these that I see many of the above practices still being perpetuated.

Yes, dancers' bodies do need to achieve extreme ranges of movement and strength if they are to have a professional career, but I do not believe that training has to be overly aggressive in order to achieve this. We now know enough about the structure and properties of the relevant tissues in the body which make up our joint and muscle units to be able to use a much more intelligent approach. Using anatomical knowledge as a key to unlock the body's potential is a much more refined and ultimately safer approach than just hitting it with a sledgehammer. It is not only the potential for physical damage to the students which is worrying about such aggressive training practices, but also the mental-emotional damage this kind of message can bring. Is it any wonder that self-punishing behaviors are common amongst dancers, particularly in the ballet world, when physically damaging behavior, reinforced by the teacher, is seen as the norm?

We have seen in previous chapters that there are a range of environmental issues stemming from infancy which can contribute to the development of self-destructive behavior patterns. So, when you consider the proportion of a young performer's life that is spent in training, often in a residential context away from his or her family support network, whilst being subjected to aggressive physical and emotional training behaviors, then we cannot fail to see the huge effect that these institutions can have on their students and the responsibility they bear in creating balanced adult performers.

One example of a self-destructive behavior pattern which is, unfortunately, often seen in the dancer population, is that of eating disorders: particularly anorexia nervosa (associated with excessive restriction of food) and bulimia nervosa (associated with bouts of binging and purging). These are psychological conditions and, as I am not a psychologist, I will just be sharing my perspective from the observational experiences I have had with both peers and patients suffering from these conditions. Let us first look at the physiological mechanisms involved in issues of disordered eating, particularly chronic under-nourishment in the female dancer population. Intensive exercise coupled with low calorie intake disrupts the normal hormonal balance and can lead to a decrease in the levels of estrogen released from the ovaries, which is necessary for regulation of the monthly cycle. Consequently, menstruation becomes either disrupted (oligomenorrhea) or shuts down entirely (secondary amenorrhea) and, if this occurs at a young enough age, menstruation may never start at all (primary amenorrhea). Low estrogen levels and poor nutrition (particularly low calcium intake) are both factors in the development of osteoporosis (low bone density), increasing the risk of stress fractures and other injuries in this population. Normally, the loading of bone during exercise, such as dancing, serves to increase bone strength, but this may be cancelled out by the debilitating effects of under nutrition. One of my peers, with whom I trained as a dancer, had suffered from anorexia since early adolescence and by the age of 28 had developed stress fractures in her spine. Her bone density was by then so low that her orthopedic consultant likened it to that of an 80 year-old. This condition can also lead to infertility or difficulty in conceiving and she had also unfortunately suffered several miscarriages when trying to start a family. Whilst I can immediately think of at least eight of my peers who, around the ages of 14 to 16, were clearly suffering from anorexic-like conditions, there were many more who would probably fall into the more general category of 'disordered eating' where they were using food as a means of controlling their environment. Research has shown that emotional stressors alone, without the added issue of disordered eating, can cause something called functional hypothalamic amenorrhea (FHA), where menstrual disturbances occur in the absence of any notable underlying pathology. A paper by Marsha D. Marcus PhD of the University of Pittsburgh showed that:

> ... women with FHA reported more dysfunctional attitudes, particularly those associated with the need for approval. [They] were more likely . . . . to endorse attitudes that are prevalent among persons vulnerable to depression, such as perfectionistic standards and concern about the judgment of others.[30]

So this tendency to menstrual disturbance may also be an issue for some in the dancer population who are not suffering from a notable eating disorder, but may be solely due to the development of the perfectionist tendencies discussed earlier in the chapter.

There is an aesthetic requirement in the world of dance, especially that of classical ballet, for a thin, lean body shape and both practice clothing and stage costumes often leave little or no place to hide. Some dance schools and companies have a 'cookie cutter' template for the required physique of their dancers, leaving little place for individualism. Anyone who doesn't conform to this model shape is seen to be substandard and therefore at risk of rejection. So young dancers are not only striving towards achieving high standards of technical proficiency, they are also striving to achieve this 'ideal' body shape in order to gain acceptance. The adolescent years, particularly for females, are a time of fluctuating body shapes as one develops into adult form, which makes this a very vulnerable time for a young dancer trying to fit their ever-changing body into a preconceived mould. In my day, it was common practice for schools to weigh and measure students at the beginning and end of every school term, ostensibly so the students could be monitored for their own welfare. However, at some training establishments, this system was wielded as a weapon, with punishments being handed out for not meeting predetermined targets. One particular dance college was notorious for actually expelling dancers from the course if they did not reach their target weight within a given time frame. Whilst the standard of dancers they produced was very high (making it an attractive place to train), this college was also notable for the number of its students suffering from disordered eating habits and, because of this, I always advised anyone whom I considered vulnerable to this condition to choose another college when considering where to train. Even at establishments where the system of weighing was not connected to any type of formal punishment, it still inevitably raised much anxiety in the dancers, who were usually already highly sensitized to their own body shape. An external stressor, such as the threat of punishment, is not necessary for inducing anxiety if the student is already conditioned to punishing themselves. When you perpetually set targets of achievement to a group with perfectionist tendencies, then they are likely to take things to extremes. To quote Dr Gabor Maté on this subject:

> The patterns of how we eat or don't eat, and how much we eat, are strongly related to the levels of stress we experience and to the coping responses we have developed in face of life's vicissitudes.[2, p.95]

This places the role of teachers, parents and dance training establishments at the heart of developing healthy attitudes towards nutrition, to ensure that appropriate relationships to food are developed in our young dancers. Failure to do so can leave the individual with an issue with which they may wrestle for the rest of their life.

In the modern world, the human body has arguably become a commodity which is only acceptable if it conforms to an 'ideal' shape – once again a comparison to a machine is made and the body is seen to be reducible to component parts: "My legs are too short", "My hips are too wide". With the rise of mechanization in the 20th century, there has been a concomitant rise in the prevalence of eating disorders – we have lost the implicit relationship with the body described by Aristotle as a "potential for the soul". We buff, polish and exercise, treating our bodies as we would a prize possession ready to be displayed as a status symbol. We project our bodies as an outward display of who we are, or perhaps who we would like people to think we are, whilst hiding our true identities behind the facade we have created. When one is in intense physical training, it is all too easy to see one's body as a tool: a series of interconnected parts disembodied from our true selves.

"Why won't my fingers move any faster on the keys?"; "Why won't my leg go any higher?" We become the puppet master of a series of moving parts, struggling desperately to retain control, as our teacher demands that we 'jump higher' or 'play louder'. We begin to approach movement from a place of tension rather than intention. Rather than allowing the movement to pass freely through the body from the root of our expressive selves, we try to grasp and manipulate it to our needs. Then, when things don't go our way, we 'blame' the body as if it had a separate identity. This detachment can lead to our feeling threatened by our bodies as they come to represent something we cannot control. When this occurs in someone already lacking in autonomy and self esteem, the result is yet more anxiety and a decreased sense of self worth. Iain McGilchrist speaks of those suffering from anorexia nervosa as having a hatred of the body and wanting it to 'disappear'. He associates this with a loss of identity, a desire for perfection and a:

> . . . need to be delivered from the contradictions and ambiguities of embodied existence.[9, p.405]

It is difficult to achieve an embodied unity in an environment of constant physical criticism, so this can result in vulnerable individuals trying to find a means of escape – to 'disappear'.

Whilst recognition of eating disorders in the dance world is thankfully now much more widespread, with many training establishments having policies in place for dealing with this issue sensitively, I do still hear some horror stories of very poor management. Just last month my advice was sought by a concerned relative whose young family member attends a very well known dance vocational school. She is apparently dangerously underweight and clearly suffering from some sort of eating disorder, which the school is handling by not allowing her to participate in dance classes until she gains a specific amount of weight. I asked if the child had also been offered any form of psychological support for her condition, but was astonished to hear that this was not the case. Whilst it may be necessary to halt a students' participation in dance training if their level of nourishment is so low that they are too weak and therefore likely to injure themselves, it is imperative that this is accompanied by additional help in the form of professional psychological and nutritional advice. To simply remove a child from class without any other form of support is to treat what is essentially self-punishing behavior with punishment. You are simply reinforcing the child's own notion that he or she has no value – you are fighting fire with fire. Eating disorders are complex psychological conditions and need to be treated with the appropriate professional support.

Let us now return to some concepts of motivation and perfectionism. Professor Dave Collins[31] of the University of Central Lancashire in the UK is an expert in the field of coaching and performance, with many published works to his name. His research into motivation has shown that perfectionism is correlated with a high quantity but low quality of motivation. However, when training focuses on developing autonomy and support, this predicts positive motivation and increased self esteem. This doesn't necessarily mean that the journey of developing young talent into competent professionals has to be all plain sailing, with no adverse experiences. In fact, the opposite is the case. He has shown that a smooth path to achievement often predicts a fall: if individuals have no experience of dealing with a stumbling block, they will not be equipped to handle such eventualities. Similarly, an early rise to success can often precede a big crash, which can be demotivating to someone for whom everything has always come easily. Stumbles, falls and road blocks are necessary in order for the student to develop the skills to handle them – in Professor Collins' words: "The bumpy road is best." However, students must also be empowered to build the necessary mental resources with which to handle these situations and this must be achieved through development of their own sense of autonomy. They must be helped to develop a positive approach to challenges and be taught how to pick themselves up and move forwards, not be punished and disparaged for having fallen in the first place. We are all familiar with the adage that we learn best from our mistakes – nobody ever learned anything by being perfect! To quote the 19th century Oxford academic and theologian Cardinal John Henry Newman:

> Nothing would be done at all if a man waited until he could do it
> so well that no one could find fault with it.[32]

Negative results are just as valuable as positive results and oftentimes more so. In the field of science and technology many great discoveries have come about when the researcher was actually looking for something altogether different: an apparent failure to achieve an intended goal actually produced a wonderfully serendipitous finding – the failure becomes a success. From the discovery of X-rays and penicillin, to microwaves and Cornflakes, there are stories of accidental findings and roundabout routes to eventual success – finding things when and where they were least expected. I'm sure we are all also familiar with the concept of trying so hard to remember something that, the more we try, the more our minds go blank – it is only when we are distracted by something completely different that it suddenly springs to mind. According to Iain McGilchrist, this is because a fixed, focused attention, (a left hemisphere trait), closes us off to the visions and memory residing in the right hemisphere. He continues:

> It is only when our intentions are fixed on something else that we
> can see things as they really are.[9, p.377]

So if training forces us to focus relentlessly on a repetitive task, this can often serve to block any progression. The trick is to go away and do something else; then you may well find the original task comes to you unbidden and with relative ease. This can explain the phenomenon that many dancers will have experienced of not being able to pull off that triple pirouette one day, but managing it with ease the next – the first time, they were probably just focusing too hard. Training, particularly in the performing arts, should not be predicated on a linear trajectory of accomplishment – after all, there are no straight lines in nature. I personally find myself very frustrated when walking in cities such as New York which have a grid-like road structure – I hate the fact that I can't invent my own route between two points and cut some corners, as it makes me feel that my creativity is being restricted. I also find it interesting that one of the main streets to buck this trend, in midtown New York, and carve its own path across the grid, is Broadway – a street which has become synonymous with the arts! If the world were to give you no choices, no forks in the road, then you would be starved of any creative expression.

So what this all amounts to is that the road to the creation of a performer needs to be a rocky one, but training should be primarily concerned with providing students with the skills to enable them to ride the bumps. Creating autonomous individuals with a balanced sense of self-worth should be the bedrock of any training, to ensure a solid emotional foundation for the physical journey. Ensuring the students are motivated by the sheer joy of their craft, rather than the fear of failure, is the route to producing healthy, well-balanced performers. It is the responsibility of both parents and teachers to support children in developing appropriate emotional boundaries, thus they will have everything they need to handle the bumps and knocks on the road ahead. In short, we should teach them to be people first. Whilst we clearly wouldn't want to dampen the dreams of aspiring young performers, there is a need to maintain a sense of reality about what the profession holds. We have to manage their expectations to ensure that their decision to choose this career is an informed one. Students need to have a balanced upbringing which does not isolate them from the 'real world' – they need the capacity to step back and take that bird's eye view, to provide them with the necessary context for the choices they make. We need to teach them that they do not have to justify their existence through a physical display of talent and that achievement is not the only way for their lives to have meaning. Introducing the concept of space, as discussed in the first chapter, both in physical terms, to help them connect to the flow of movement through the body without tension, and also in terms of time, so that they don't view their training as a race to the finishing line, will also be helpful to both their physical and emotional development. We need to dispel the notion that faster is better and allow them the space to progress at their own rate without endless comparison to those around them. Hans Selye advises that:

> *The great art is to express our vitality through the particular chan-*
> *nels and at the particular speed which Nature foresaw for us.*[1, p.419]
> (original italics).

Nature speaks to us through our bodies and only those who have learned to listen will master this valuable art. Only when you are truly connected to your body will you be able to receive and interpret the amazing gift of wisdom that is held within. Supporting the development of autonomous individuals with a strong sense of their embodied selves should be the ultimate aim of all performing arts training. I close this chapter with the words of the German philosopher Martin Heidegger:

> Anyone can achieve their fullest potential, who we are might be predetermined, but the path we follow is always of our own choosing. We should never allow our fears or the expectations of others to set the frontiers of our destiny.[33]

6

The relationship between body language and authenticity

So much of what connects performers to their audience is communicated via the medium of body language. Dance is arguably all body language and even for an instrumental musician the interaction between the instrument and the human body depicts a subtext of that interrelationship, as well as the musicians' relationship to the repertoire. If one watches a film of both an amateur and a professional musician with the sound muted, one knows immediately which is which: the ease with which a professional interacts with the instrument communicates a confidence to the audience, allowing them to sit back, relax and enjoy the performance. As I mentioned in the first chapter, I also believe that body postures (and therefore body language) can be 'heard' through changes of resonance and tone in an instrumental musician, so here we can see a connection between body language and both the eye and the ear. It is only when these visual, aural and, for actors and singers, vocal signals are all in unison that an authentic message is portrayed. Before we look a little deeper into the role of body language in the performing arts, let us first explore the developmental, physiological and cultural origins of body language and its place in human communication.

In Chapter 2, we discussed the notion of social bonding being a vital component of the survival of the species and, in pre-linguistic times, body language, touch and grooming formed the basis of all communication. Our primitive ancestors were highly successful and well organised long before spoken language had evolved – the fact that we are still here today is a ringing endorsement for the efficacy of body language. As social groups began to spread geographically, it is thought that music first evolved in the form of intonations and rhythms in order to allow communication at a distance. This was a development of body language and touch, meaning our musical roots are firmly based in embodied communication. Young infants communicate first with body movements and then with changes in vocal pitch and intonation before vocabulary and syntax begin to be overlaid on these vocal shapes, echoing our evolutionary roots.

So, if body language stems from primitive communication methods in early humans, is there a 'universal body language' that crosses all cultures or are there regional differences, just as for spoken language? Opinions on this have changed throughout history, with Charles Darwin first suggesting that facial expressions of emotions were cross-cultural,[34] followed by a group of researchers in the 1950s suggesting that there were no innate patterns of this kind.[35] Then in the 1960s, another group of American researchers, who conducted extensive studies across three continents, supported the Darwinian view that there were indeed some basic commonalities of expression across all cultures.[36] The view held today is that there are some basic expressions that could be correctly read and interpreted by anyone in any part of the world. They include happiness, sadness, fear, anger, surprise and disgust. In our earlier exploration of some of the physiological responses to emotions such as fear and anger, which may increase our heart rate, raise our blood pressure etc., it makes sense that these physical reactions are also a part of the telegraphing of these emotional states.

However, beyond these basic emotional expressions, there are indeed many regional differences in how we communicate with our bodies. For instance in India, a shake of the head means 'yes' and a nod of the head means 'no', in opposition to Western cultures. There are also cultural differences in the acceptable levels of eye contact, touch and space. How long you should hold eye contact with a stranger before it is considered impolite can vary with geography: British or American tourists in France or Italy may find themselves shifting uncomfortably in their seat on the train under the gaze of a local. In Arab cultures, physical proximity and touching are considered normal, even amongst strangers in a public place where pushing and jostling are commonplace, and hand holding between men is also seen as a sign of affection and without any sexual connotation. Such behaviors in other countries may be considered a gross invasion of personal boundaries. In these instances, body language can be as foreign to us as an unfamiliar spoken language can be. However, if you understand the cultural rules, then misunderstandings can be avoided.

It is often said that body language cannot lie, which has led to its being used to 'read' people under interrogation and also gives rise to that subliminal feeling we may experience when something someone is saying just doesn't 'add up'. The limbic system is the part of our brain which deals, amongst other things, with emotions, the fight or flight mechanism, and pleasure. It is thought to be older than areas such as the frontal cortex, which is responsible for language, and therefore is the seat of our earliest forms of communication. Animals interact with us via their limbic systems and are much more acutely in touch with this area than humans who, in the modern world, tend to identify more readily with their 'rational' minds. The responses from our limbic system are hard-wired and not under our conscious control, and it is from here that our body language arises. This links with the earlier concept of those basic emotional expressions which are universal: if they arise from our limbic system and are therefore subconscious, then they will remain unaltered by learned cultural stereotypes.

Studies have shown that up to 90% of human communication is non-verbal, which necessitates the question of why we needed to develop language at all. There are varying theories on this, but one proposed by Iain McGilchrist suggests that language developed as a means to manipulate our world. He says that language enables us to name things and that:

> Naming things gives us power over them, so that we can use them.[9, p.114]

Language also expands our capacity for memory and planning, both valuable tools in the battle to control our environment. Although animals have been shown to demonstrate the capacity for deceit, the development of language clearly vastly improves our ability to lie and manipulate, which may be driven by a need for power and possession. If we remind ourselves that lack of control is considered one of the most potent stressors to our physiology, then we can see how this need to gain power over our environment might have arisen. So if language can so readily distort the truth, then it is our instinctive, unconscious body language that can unmask the deception. The British physician and primatologist, John Napier, wrote of the symbolic nature of gesture:

> If language was given to men to conceal their thoughts, then gesture's purpose was to disclose them.[37, p.166]

So this leads to the concept that our emotional reality and our verbal reality can sometimes be at odds and, when this is the case, the message projected will necessarily be inauthentic. From an audience's perspective, the ears will hear one thing, but the eyes will see another and their Limbic systems will sniff out the deception. McGilchrist takes this further by relating it to the concepts of left and right hemispheric differences in the brain. The right hemisphere is involved in emotional expressivity via the face, the voice and body postures and is more accurate in reading and interpreting the emotions on the faces of others than the left. It is also the mediator of spontaneous facial expressions and the expression of sadness through tears – another physiological manifestation of our emotional state. The right hemisphere controls the left side of the face (known as the left hemiface) and McGilchrist says that it is here that we display most of our emotional expression. He continues:

> Emotions are also more strongly perceived when expressed by the left hemiface: and, intriguingly, the left hemiface is also larger than the right in right-handers.[9, p.61]

(As you rush to your mirror to check this, remember that the mirror reverses the view!). He also highlights the preference for mothers to cradle their infants to the left, therefore exposing the left hemiface to most immediate view. This tendency is thought to be universal, dating back thousands of years, and is also evident in gorillas and chimpanzees. The right hemisphere is also thought to be better at reading expression from the eyes, while the left hemisphere ignores the eyes in favor of the lower half of the face and mouth. Without the expressivity of the eyes, it is much harder to read someone's emotions – we are less able to tell if a smile is genuine if we cannot also see the eyes. I spoke in Chapter 2 about performers becoming unduly mechanistic if they have become stuck in the left-brained mode of learning, and have disconnected from the expressivity of the right; so here we can see how this could also be read via their facial expressions and body language. The left hemisphere is also connected to forced or willed expressions, lacking the spontaneity of the right. This is significant to those performers who are playing a role – if one approaches an expression by trying to break it down to component parts then piecing together a 'look', the result is likely to be a willed expression which will be interpreted by an audience as inauthentic. One has to be able to tap into one's own vault of genuine experiences in order to produce an authentic facial expression, and it is the right hemisphere which holds the key to our emotional memory.

Moving on from the expressions of the face, what is the connection between the words we speak and the gestures we make with our hands and arms? Language and gesture, particularly that of pointing and grasping with the right hand, have a neuroanatomical connection due to the proximity of the areas responsible for these actions in the brain. A region of the frontal lobe, known as Broca's area, is linked to the production of language, but is also linked to the interpretation of gestures in others. When we consider the aforementioned concept that gesture or body language predates spoken language, many authors now believe that Broca's area began by translating the movements of others into abstract ideas and then continued by associating sounds with these abstract meanings, therefore connecting them to spoken language. So if the construction of our language, as discussed earlier, is a function of the left hemisphere and therefore conscious and willed, how do we juxtapose this with the notion of body language as arising from the unconscious mind? A fascinating study from 1985 by the American scientist Benjamin Libet, a pioneer in the field of the human consciousness, casts some doubt on the notion of conscious willed motion – that is, that we 'decide' consciously to initiate a motion, then carry it out. By the use of electrodes on the scalp, he was able to measure the brain activity of a group of 40 individuals who were asked to make spontaneous finger movements. One of the things he measured was the 'Readiness Potential' (RP) – this is an anticipatory signal that occurs in the motor cortex before any voluntary (or consciously willed) muscle movements are initiated. The subjects were asked to record the moment they felt the urge to move their finger (conscious thought) and then the movement itself was recorded via an Electromyograph (EMG) of the appropriate muscle. What the study showed was that the RP occurred not just before the movement had been initiated, as would be expected, but about 500 milliseconds prior to the conscious decision to act – the unconscious mind knew what was about to happen before the person had made the conscious decision to move. In Libet's words:

> The present experimental findings provide direct evidence that unconscious processes can and do initiate voluntary action and point to a definable cerebral basis for this unconscious function.[38]

It is not that he is challenging the notion that we have free will, but that we must broaden our concept of what constitutes free will to include our subconscious mind.

Iain McGilchrist[9, p.190] points to further evidence in this field, in particular to the work of David McNeill who, through his detailed work from video tape evidence of human interaction, showed, amongst many other things, that gesture slightly anticipates speech. A subconsciously driven physical movement, mediated by the right hemisphere, occurs before the spoken word is formulated: then as the person begins to construct the thought into language and to speak, the left hemisphere takes over the execution of the gesture and describes the thought. It has also been shown that restricting the arm movements of someone who is speaking actually has a negative effect on the fluency of the speech, demonstrating that the gestures are not just a reflection of the words, but are an integral part of the formulation of speech itself. In McNeill's words:

> . . . gestures do not merely reflect thought, but help constitute thought.[39]

His experiments also showed that when there is a mismatch between gesture and speech, it is the gesture that is correct in 100% of cases. Gesture does not lie even when speech does. This thought is echoed by Julius Fast in his book entitled Body Language when he says:

> If the spoken language is stripped away and the only communication left is body language, the truth will find some way of poking through. Spoken language itself is a great obscurer.[40]

So the subconscious mind and right hemisphere have primacy over our conscious thoughts and actions, and are the initiators of our so-called voluntary or consciously willed movements. The left hemisphere, however, is capable of overriding these signals and changing the message, but there will always be an inherent, subliminal 'tell' in the milliseconds before the conscious mind takes over.

Having explored how our body language and spoken word are produced, we must now take a look at how these signals are read by the interpreter or, in the world of performance, the audience. I mentioned above that the right hemisphere is involved in the reading of the emotional expressions of another individual, particularly of the eyes, and Broca's area translates the movements of others into ideas and then language. This area also contains what have become known colloquially as 'mirror neurones'. These are neurones which fire not just when we ourselves act, but also when we observe the actions of others. When we watch the hand movements of another person, our neurones 'mirror' the same motor activity pattern, although the actual end movement is not produced – at a neural level, it is as if we were doing it ourselves. This is thought, by some neurologists, to enable us to understand the intentions and goals of others, to learn through imitation and perhaps to provide us with the basis for empathy. It is postulated that a deficiency in this system may be linked to autism, where empathic understanding is often absent, although this is still speculative. Listening passively to music has also been shown to activate pre-motor areas of the brain, indicating a form of planning for action connected with the listening experience. How often have you found yourself unconsciously tapping your fingers or feet along with a piece of music, or beginning to follow the movements of a dancer from your seat in the theatre? Perhaps now we can start to see the evolutionary roots for this tendency to embody and understand the world around us.

This brings us on to the role of empathy and imitation in our evolution. Both are thought to be essential to our survival in terms of social cohesion. The premise that 'together we are stronger' has allowed us to develop as a species and to acquire the dominant position we appear to hold in the world. The ability to experience empathy allows us to better understand those around us and to have a clearer idea of their intentions, therefore promoting social bonding. Imitation is a means to acquire new skills and, when combined with an empathic approach involving the neurological systems previously discussed, it can be a means to truly embody and identify with the subject being imitated, thereby producing an authentic result. This is seen as distinct from 'copying' which is a purely mechanistic exercise of breaking actions down and reproducing them. Imitation was used by early hunters, who would 'become' the animal they were tracking in order to be successful, and it is also the way in which children learn to develop new skills – they don't just copy, they become. The ability to share empathically and learn skills from others by imitation promotes survival of the species. The aspiration for skill acquisition is usually driven by a respect for the people being imitated – a desire to 'be like them' – and although the learning of skills may be seen to be by its nature competitive, if the ultimate goal is to improve the species as a whole, then are we really as competitive a species as we sometimes paint ourselves? Perhaps it is only when we begin to identify with acquisitional goals such as money or notoriety that we stray from our true evolutionary path. The breakdown of families and societies, with the increasing spread of urbanisation, would seem to reflect this shift from group-driven activities to more individualistic trajectories where it is 'every man for himself'. Music and dance have also followed this trend, with the media driving endless competitions where rivalry is championed and contestants are lured with the promise of fame and fortune, which completely overlooks the inherent non-competitive nature of art. When it comes to imitation, we should be careful about which models we choose as, in McGilchrist's words:

> ... as a species, not only as individuals, we will become what we imitate.[9, p.253]

The more we 'copy' for reasons of material gain, the less individual we will become. Only when we use our imagination, and all those right hemisphere traits of emotional memory and expression in the process of imitation, will we retain our individuality. If we are led by the mechanistic and acquisitive approach of the left hemisphere, we are in danger of becoming clones!

So let us now explore the role of body language in the performance domain, in terms both of the connection with the audience and the authenticity of the messages produced and received. The specific performance environment is clearly a factor here in terms of the proximity of the audience to the players. In a large theatre, for instance, there will necessarily be a greater distance between the performers and the audience, whereas a close-up shot on the big screen in film leaves little place to hide. When performers are on the stage, their gestures may need to be exaggerated or stylized to be telegraphed through the Proscenium Arch to the back of the theatre and will therefore be necessarily more symbolic than literal. This is particularly of note in the absence of the spoken word, such as in Ballet 'mime'. This distance can also be useful to create illusions, preventing an audience from seeing the mechanics involved in the production. However, in a close-up shot on film, the slightest twitch of a facial muscle can be writ large across the screen, meaning any inauthentic movement or gesture will be clearly exposed to view. The key to authenticity is to ensure that any facial expression, gesture or movement is truly reflective of the verbal message being spoken or emotion being expressed: as we have seen, trying to mechanistically replicate this through analysis and reconstruction is likely to end up with an unconvincing result – a left-brained replication. The self-awareness of an actor who tries to dissect the work and then reconstruct it, may render his or her performance inauthentic. The actor cannot be visible in the process or the illusion is lost. We return to the idea of art being a dialogue with an audience, not a monologue to the audience. If the audience is not immersed in the experience and is aware of the machinations, they will be just observers, not participants. Iain McGilchrist talks of the embarrassment and discomfort of watching bad acting saying:

> It draws our attention to the fact that the actors are acting, and to how they see themselves; they become like critics whose self-preening causes them to obtrude between us and what they claim to illuminate. The implicit becomes explicit and all is lost.[9, p.184]

Art needs to be transparent – the actors and scenery are there to lead the audience through to something other. The moment the scenery wobbles or the actor stumbles, the transparency is lost and the members of the audience merely become spectators again.

In the world of film, actors must retain this transparency despite being surrounded by all the crew members and technical paraphernalia, which can be very distracting and can lack the intimacy and context of a theatre set. Spontaneity must also be maintained despite sometimes having to repeat the same scene many times. Barbra Streisand, speaking about her time on the set of the 1973 film, *The Way We Were*, which demanded high levels of emotion throughout, says about the acting process that it is:

> . . . not intellectual. You only work at method digging when it's unnatural, when it's difficult. But if something feels totally natural, you just let it be, you let it flow. You're like the vessel that this thing works through . . . It's a lot in the subconscious, the unconscious, it's not an intellectual thing. You do it out of instinct and the feeling of something, then intellectualize it later . . . The camera knows if it's preconceived.[41]

This echoes a right-brained approach, drawing upon existing emotions without bringing in the scrutiny of the rational mind in order to retain authenticity and realism, something for which she is highly renowned and clearly very adept. Research has shown that our emotions have primacy over our reason, meaning that we first make an intuitive assessment of a situation before we layer it with cognitive reasoning, rather than just using emotions as an embellishment for rational thought. When an actor follows this natural path in the creation of a character, then she or he is more likely to achieve an authentic result.

So, when witnessing a truly authentic performance, to what, or to where are the audience being taken? I spoke in earlier chapters about art being based in a sense of longing – a reaching out to something beyond ourselves but to which we are already somehow implicitly connected. From the writings of Plato to the work of Carl Jung, there have been theories of a 'collective unconscious' or 'universal knowledge' that somehow connects all of humankind. More recent work by George Lakoff and Mark Johnson in their book *Philosophy in the Flesh: The Embodied Mind and Its Challenge to Western Thought*, proposes the notion that our mind, and therefore our cognition, are dependent upon our sensorimotor system and emotions – that our perceptual and motor systems actually help to shape some of our basic concepts, and that these are then necessarily common across cultures.

> The mind is not merely embodied, but embodied in such a way that our conceptual systems draw largely upon the commonalities of our bodies and of the environments we live in. The result is that much of a person's conceptual system is either universal or widespread across languages and cultures.[42]

This resonates with the aforementioned work by Libet, who found that movement is initiated before the conscious thought to do so arises. So, perhaps these theories all point to some implicit context to which we are all fundamentally linked and which we 'feel' or 'intuit', rather than just understand in a cognitive sense. With the added effect of our mirror neurones providing a means for our motor systems to tap into this context when we are purely observing, we begin to see the circularity that can be formed. When an artist provides the conduit for the audience to tap into this reciprocal implicitness, then we have authenticity.

So for actors in the theatre who must repeat the same dialogue night after night, how do they ensure that their performance remains fresh and new, and not just a mechanical regurgitation? In order to memorize the lines and the blocking (the actor's choreography around the stage), one will need to have engaged in left-brained categorization for this memorization to occur. However, if we recall that emotional memory is held in the right hemisphere, it is to this that the actor must return to ensure the performance remains a unique, original experience each time. Spontaneity cannot be willed, so the more focused attention that we bring to such things as emotion, which are, by nature, implicit, the more we are likely to destroy them. To dissect an emotion requires the kind of self-awareness that renders the actor opaque and visible which, as was discussed above, serves to disconnect him or her from the audience. According to Iain McGilchrist:

> Too much self-awareness destroys not just spontaneity, but the quality that makes things live; the performance of music or dance, of courtship, love and sexual behaviour, humour, artistic creation and religious devotion become mechanical, lifeless, and may grind to a halt if we are too self aware.[9, p.180]

In order for an actor to achieve this spontaneity, it is also vital that the playwright creates characters who are believable and authentic to begin with. Before the works of Shakespeare, much of dramatic art had been more about producing 'copies' of real people and representations of situations with which an audience would connect on a more cognitive level. Shakespeare's skill was in creating real flesh and blood individuals, which allowed the audience to connect with them on a more subconscious emotional level. The dialogue does not just rely on the left hemisphere skills of reproduction, but is grown from the roots of right hemispherical emotional memory. This echoes the natural order of our own emotional expression, from implicit to explicit, and is therefore in harmony with it, allowing the audience to become one with the performers.

Costume also plays a vital role in authenticity and not just in 'representing' the appropriate look for the sake of the audience. For performers too, the costume can be a conduit to the embodiment of the character they are playing. If we return to the concept of the primitive hunter who would 'become' the animal he was hunting, this was often achieved by the wearing of the animal skin itself to aid the process. Tribal dances would also involve mimicry of the animal's movements, whilst the dancer was adorned with the animal skins, to evoke the spirit of the beast and become one with it. So, too, the costumes of the theatre help performers to become the characters they are playing. As a dancer who worked in many different genres and styles, I would always find it strange performing a particular dance style were I not wearing the appropriate attire. Trying to do street jazz in ballet clothing

127

and shoes would just feel completely wrong and I would find myself less able to create authentic moves. Julius Fast also speaks of another aspect of costume wearing which enables a kind of freedom that would otherwise be difficult for someone to achieve. He calls this 'Double Masking' where the wearing of one mask allows us to drop another:

> The man who dresses up in a clown suit for some amateur theatri-
> cal production often sheds his inhibitions as he dons his costume,
> and he is able to cavort and joke and 'clown around' with perfect
> looseness and freedom.[40, p.76]

The costume relieves us of the perceived need to conform and allows us to truly 'unmask'. Although we talk about actors wearing masks of performance, is it actually the case that they are using a mask in their 'real life' persona and the theatrical masks of costume bestow upon them the freedom to reveal their true selves? Perhaps the actor is never more authentic than when he or she is on the stage and it is in the real world where the mask is in place. The mask may give one the freedom to convey emotions that one is otherwise unable to express.

On the stage, a play will normally follow a logical chronological course, allowing the actor to become the character at the start and to follow it through to the end of the story. In film, however, scenes are rarely filmed in chronological order and, in contrast to the natural flow of a theatrical production, actors will have to deal with the stop/ start nature of cinematography. As it is often the case that only one camera is being used, the actor may have to repeat sections of script many times, to be filmed from several different angles, but each must be an exact replica of the first in order to avoid issues of continuity. This therefore differs from the earlier notion of each performance of a line being a uniquely individual experience to ensure authenticity. With the camera often literally making the actor larger than life, high levels of exactness are required which may limit the actor's freedom to express. My own experience of this came when, after spending many years in theatre where 'larger than life' expression was the norm, I was cast in an episode of a TV series where I suddenly found myself in a very different world. In one scene I had to spot someone in the distance, register a look of shock, then say a line all whilst in a very tight head-shot. The director had me repeat this several times as he kept saying that my head was moving too much, although I thought I was holding it perfectly still. I found it so difficult to appear spontaneously shocked whilst in a self-enforced headlock – it just felt so unnatural. Knowing what I do now about gesture preceding thought and actually serving to construct the thought itself, and the concept that restricting gesture has been shown to restrict fluency of language, it is no wonder that I found this rather difficult. So, film actors are often having to work within very tight boundaries regarding gesture, and also have to be ready to switch their character on and off at will every time the director shouts 'action' or 'cut', whilst often recording scenes completely out of chronological sequence. This is all done under the very close scrutiny of the camera with the images then being blown up to huge proportions to be displayed on a large movie screen.

Retaining authenticity in these circumstances requires a high degree of talent and skill. It is no wonder then that some actors favor acting approaches where they draw on their own emotional experiences to identify with the character they are portraying and often completely embody their character for the duration of the project whilst both on set and off. This gives them a constancy and flow to help to navigate the often chaotic nature of the filming process whilst retaining the authenticity of their character. From the perspective of health, however, how far one takes this embodiment of a character is likely to be reflected in one's own physiology to a certain extent. If one is playing Mary Poppins, the experience may be a positively uplifting one, but if one is playing a darkly psychotic serial killer, the effects may be a little more damaging! If you are, for instance, playing a highly stressed individual and you are truly expressing emotions from your own vaults of experience, you will also be experiencing the cascade of chemical and neurological reactions that are a fundamental part of that process. You will be experiencing true physiological symptoms which, although a fundamental part of the authenticity of your performance, also represent withdrawals from that irreplaceable tank of adaptation energy, as mentioned in Chapter 3. If you are also carrying these emotions with you in your personal life for the duration of the filming process, then the effects can be profound. That is not to say that we should prevent actors from giving authentic performances, or they will end up making themselves ill. However, they should be made aware of the physical price being paid, and ensure that they give their bodies the necessary rest and recuperation to balance the output. If you keep pushing the limits without respite, burnout may follow. There are other, more outside/in approaches to acting that may afford the actor the ability to step away from their character more easily. I merely suggest that the actor look beyond the artistic outcome of an approach towards the physiological ramifications and take steps to ensure a healthy balance is maintained.

For those performers who have developed the ability to escape into or to hide behind inauthentic versions of themselves as a childhood coping mechanism, this skill of jumping in and out of character in performance may come quite naturally. However, Dr Gabor Maté gives a caution about the expression of emotions in performance:

> Artistic expression by itself is only a form of acting out emotions, not a way of working them through.[2, p.26]

Some performers may be highly skilled at dissecting the emotional journey of their character, but may not afford their own personal journey the same level of scrutiny. They run the risk of becoming a terminal escapee from their own history, jumping from character to character whilst never getting to know their true selves and we have already seen the risks this may pose to their own health and wellbeing.

Throughout their career, actors may need to play many roles and versatility is often key to survival in the industry. However, some actors may find themselves playing the same role for many years, for example in a long-running TV drama. So how does this affect their ability to remain truly authentic? Do some of the character's traits and behaviors inevitably rub off? To help me to understand more about this particular aspect of an actor's experience, I turned to my friend and actor, Stefan Dennis. Stef has played the role of Paul Robinson in the long-running Australian drama serial *Neighbours* on and off for some 29 years, so he has great experience of these issues. He generously took the time during his extremely hectic filming schedule to respond to my questions on the subject of how one maintains a separation between one's character and one's own self when playing the same role for many years, and how one is affected by the physical and emotional traits of one's character, particularly when the character is not always the nicest guy in town! Here are his thoughts:

A question I get asked too often, particularly in press interviews, is how easily I shake off my character after shooting for a day in studio or location. The answer in my case is 'very easily'. I have played quite intense characters on stage and have found it much harder to step away from the character I have just been immersed in for the previous two hours or so. When an actor is portraying a character in a play or stage musical they are inside the story from beginning to end and therefore 'become' the character to the point where sometimes the audience is not there. I remember playing the part of Mickey in *Blood Brothers* in the West End, London. As the play/musical progressed, Mickey became darker and more intense and emotional, therefore by the time I reached my dressing room after the show I could sometimes be an emotional wreck (I know . . . pussy actors!). However, I discovered this was not necessarily a bad thing. It was actually a way of releasing myself from my character. I would then sit quietly for ten or fifteen minutes and take off my make-up and wind down. The opposite takes place when I am playing Paul Robinson (a character I have played on and off over the last 29 years). The reason for this is that when we are filming a studio day we do not film chronologically and, therefore, do not get to see the story from beginning to end. Also in between 'takes', particularly when shooting a dramatic or emotional scene, there is usually a bit of joking around. From an outsiders point of view this may be perceived as unprofessional, but in actual fact it is again a method of releasing the tension that may otherwise build up from portraying a roller coaster of emotions in a day. Which gets me back to the reason I say it is easy for me to shake off the character after a day's filming. In truth, I generally get out of character when the Director shouts "Cut"!

Though I'm not a huge fan of 'Method' acting, I can certainly see its merits. I like to think of those immortal words from Laurence Olivier to Dustin Hoffman when the younger actor had been reportedly living it rough in the park for some days in preparation for his role in *Marathon Man* . . . "Haven't you ever heard of 'acting', dear boy?" I quote this because there is definitely an argument for both sides. But as an actor working on an ongoing drama serial, the need to 'act' rather than 'become' is essential. I, for example, play a character who is constantly barking at people and often grumpy. If I was to hang onto these traits, I don't think I would last too long with my friends and family, who know me as otherwise. So, whereas it is not so good to take character traits to your normal life, it can be advantageous to do the opposite. For example, we, as actors, are called upon to come up with a range of emotions in a filming day and because we don't shoot in sequence and the rate of filming is so fast, I tend to draw on things from my life, or from what I have witnessed, to come up with these emotions in a convincing way.

When I was a younger actor, I found it very difficult to cry on cue, or show a deep-seated sadness or, indeed, absolute joy in a scene, given the time frame we had to work in. As I matured, both as an actor and in my personal life, together with becoming a father, I have found it much easier to 'come up with the goods' in a scene, because I now have so much more to draw on. We quite often hear how a younger singer doesn't have the emotion or feeling behind a song simply because they haven't lived life yet. The same applies to acting. We can go to acting schools and workshops until the cows come home, but until the actor has experienced things in life, there will always be a certain void in the performance. Don't get me wrong, I'm not being derogatory towards acting schools and drama classes as these are an essential part of an actor's training, in order to be able to portray life and experience convincingly. I'm simply saying that training, together with life's experiences make the actor's toolbox more complete.

So hopefully, you can see why I find it important not to hang on to the psychological side of a character for longer than needed. I have worked with actors who have insisted on being their character both on and off set during filming breaks. Though this can be good and necessary for the actor to be able to slot straight back into the role, it can be confusing to the people around them, as they are not sure who to address and how carefully to tread. Bit of 'Jekyll and Hyde' going on in the real world . . . I think. But again, I do see the sense in holding on to the character during filming breaks or intervals (in the quiet of their trailer or dressing room) when doing a particularly demanding role in a film or stage play.

Apart from the psychological aspects, there can be physical traits that have to be introduced into the role. For example, the character may have a bad injury or perhaps a defect from birth or otherwise. It is very helpful if the actor can draw on experiences for this physical side. I'm not suggesting actors should go out and break a few bones or contract serious illnesses in order to be able to portray physical attributes, but there are a couple of avenues open: 1) being able to recall what a certain pain or discomfort feels like because of an injury or illness to you; 2) in cases where an actor is playing someone with a physical trait or personality disorder that is far removed from the way the actor really is, we have the ability in most cases to be able to research these traits. A superb example of this is Leonardo Di Caprio's role, playing a mentally handicapped kid in *What's Eating Gilbert Grape*.

Looking at the physical side can backfire, unfortunately. I speak from experience in at least two instances. In my opinion, one of the West End and Broadway dream roles for an actor is the part of Mickey in *Blood Brothers*. Mickey starts out in the first half as a seven year old boy, and as the play progresses so, too, does his age. Apart from the epic emotional journey the character goes through, the physical side is very demanding. You can imagine, adults playing children, then teenagers and so on. When I landed the role, I threw myself into it wholeheartedly in order to give the performance the respect it deserved. In doing so I watched little kids . . . a lot. (I'm sure there were some people thinking, "Why is that bloke over there looking at those kids in the playground . . . ? Dirty perv!"). This not only gave me the genuine chance to revisit the mental attitude of little kids, but also to pick up the absolute and energetically physical side. Put together with the wonderful direction of Bob Thompson, I was soon leaping and bounding all over the stage during the show. Unfortunately, even though my mental and physical energy remained trapped in that of a seven year old, my real body was facing its mid thirties. So as the saying goes "Something had to give!" and, sure enough, nine months into the run on the West End my back had had enough. Several weeks of chiropractic and osteopathic manipulation started to correct things. But it meant the role of Mickey, for me, was to become 'something I once did'.

The other experience was more recent and centers around my current and ongoing role in the drama serial, *Neighbours*. Some years ago, the producers decided it would be a novel idea to lop off my character's right leg, just below the knee. So, wanting to give the journey of the leg loss, subsequent rehabilitation and living with this handicap a real truth,

I decided to do a fair amount of research into amputation, rehabilitation and living/coping with a prosthetic leg. I felt this was extremely necessary, as it was not just a storyline that would last a short time, but it was to be a character trait that would last for the duration of my time in the show. To aid the realism in my character's gait, I had an orthopedic splint made, which would keep everything rigid, and give the appearance of walking with a fake leg. Although I have to say, at this point, a lot of people ask why I wasn't limping in an episode they had watched or "Do you ever forget to limp?", which amuses me because one of the things I noticed during my research of prosthetic limbs is that it is hardly noticeable with someone who has become accustomed to wearing one.

After wearing the splint in and around the studios for a couple of years, I noticed I was getting pain in my heel. Some X-rays and treatments later it was discovered that I had developed a spur on my heel which was directly linked to the wearing of the splint for an extended period. This was an ailment that took a good year to remedy with ultrasound and chiropractic treatments. Needless to say, I no longer wear the splint and have resorted back to good old 'acting' to portray a convincing but subtle gait.

So you can see how, in some instances, the need to act a physical trait convincingly can end up as a case of life imitating art.

I am very grateful to Stef for sharing these wonderful insights on how an actor deals with the physical and emotional journeys of his characters, and how his own personal experiences in life are a vital part of being able to authentically portray a role. He also highlighted some good examples of how an actor can often pay a physical price for his dedication to a role.

We will now turn to the subject of emotional expression through the medium of dance. Here there is clearly an absence of spoken language, so the body is the only means of communication and, as we have seen, research literature supports the concept that bodily expression and gesture are always truthful. The well-known contemporary dancer and choreographer Martha Graham is known to have said of dance that it is:

... the hidden language of the soul of the body

and adds that:

The body never lies.[43]

Before the advent of spoken language, all we had with which to communicate were our bodies, so body language is at the root of all that we are. We are embodied beings and dance is a fundamental means of expression to which everyone is connected – we are wired that way. I am always surprised when someone says to me "I can't dance," or "I wish I could dance" – if dance is just an expression of emotion through movement, then it is something of which we are all capable. What those people are really saying is that they feel unable to produce the socially and culturally acceptable forms of dance which society has decided meet some artificially constructed criteria. The high levels of self-awareness that we have developed, particularly in the Western world, often serve to cut us off from our primal roots – we saw above how too much self-awareness destroys spontaneity. We are identifying with a left-brained list of socially acceptable behaviors, which tend to be disparaging of any right-brained emotive expression that falls outside these criteria. We adhere to strict social and cultural rules, which serve to disconnect us from so much of our natural embodied expression, and encounter criticism should we dare to step outside the lines. Dance is only acceptable when it falls into the classifications that society has set and certain standards have to be met for someone to be deemed a competent dancer. If you fall below these standards then you are likely to be labeled as having 'two left feet' and discouraged from continuing. We deem those cultures who still maintain tribal dance as a core part of their traditions to be somehow beneath us, or behind us developmentally, and we would be highly suspicious, or even horrified, if we discovered that our neighbors were undertaking such practices in their back yard each night. However, if we place this tribal dance in a theatre or exhibition, then it becomes acceptable. If we turn it into a commodity, then we have found a place for it, and it has a value with which we are more comfortable. This is where society can be wearing a communal mask which serves to disconnect us from our true selves – we are all upholding and conforming to an artificial rule about the limits of acceptability for embodied self expression. Without this conduit for emotional expression, the result can be repression, and we have seen the physiological effects that this can bring. Is it any wonder then that the Western world is so afflicted with stress-related disorders?

Let us now explore the connection between music and dance and the role that body language plays here. If you ask most professional dancers what is at the very root of their drive to express themselves through dance, many of them will say it is the music. In saying this, though, we need to be clear about the true definition of music. Following the themes in the above paragraph about what are deemed to be the socially acceptable parameters for dance, music too is prone to this need for cultural categorization. However, this serves to limit our concept of what music really encompasses. Music can be anything from a rhythm tapped out with a foot, which does not have to conform to any of our modern constructs of acceptable patterns, to a full panoply of synchronized instruments, but all of these require human movement. Music cannot exist without human movement – they are inextricably linked in both practical and neurological terms. Iain McGilchrist says:

> Music is deeply gestural in nature: dance and the body are everywhere implied in it. Even when we do not move, music activates the brain's motor cortex.[9, p.119]

As was mentioned before, when our primitive ancestors spread geographically and were no longer able to see the bodily communication upon which they usually relied, music was used to telegraph these messages over distances. But these messages were not just being communicated by sounds, the listener would be visualizing the movements that the sender had made with his or her body in the process of producing that sound and it is through the embodiment of these sounds by the listener that the message is understood. The listener would be feeling what he or she had heard and reading the physiological messages produced by his or her own body. One can even go so far as to say that music and movement are indistinguishable. Accordingly, there is also no dividing line between movement and dance, except those lines artificially inserted by certain cultures, so therefore music and dance are also one and the same. Although most traditional and professional forms of dance are set to music, in the world of contemporary dance there are some choreographic pieces that have no musical accompaniment. However, that is not to say that they too are not based in music. I have performed some such pieces myself and although there may have been no audible music, I would very definitely have created my own music which was playing through my body. Even in the absence of any melodic overtones, I would have a definite rhythm for the dance I was performing and, when working in a group piece, this integral rhythm is essential for coordinating and synchronizing with the other dancers. You 'feel' the communal rhythm, to which you are all linked, rather than hear it. Without it, there would be no cohesion and partnered lifts would become rather treacherous! In such works, the dancers are exploiting all those deep primal means of communication, and I personally found it incredible how much could be said and understood using these methods.

So, if music and dance are such an integral part of who we are as human beings, then, fundamentally, we are all musicians and dancers. Those who would disagree with that statement have either just become cut off from their implicit ancestral foundations, or have been duped by the narrow classifications for what constitutes music and dance in our modern culture. Those who have chosen to turn music and dance into their profession are probably just a little more in touch with, and therefore driven by, those fundamental roots. When I hear music, I feel compelled to move – I find it hard to sit still and will at least be drumming a finger or tapping a foot, even when social propriety prevents me from flinging myself around bodily! The fact that I became a professional dancer is probably because I followed this very strong instinct to an extreme degree – I couldn't ignore it. I even classify music by the degree to which it makes me want to move. My definition of 'good' music, or to use a less judgmental description, 'music with which I resonate', is based on the degree to which it inspires me to choreograph. Moderately enjoyable music may give me the urge to get up and dance, but when I really connect with a piece, I begin to spontaneously create more definite choreography in my head – I am physically recreating the message the composer has written, just as our primitive ancestors did. When I choreograph professionally, the music is the most essential component for me, and when the music is right, the creative process requires little or no conscious thought – I just hit the ground running! If, however, I have been asked to choreograph to a pre-selected piece of music for which I feel little or no connection, then the process becomes rather different. I literally have to construct the choreography piece by piece and often find myself hitting roadblocks. Here we can clearly see how, in the first instance, my choreography is mediated by the right hemisphere, the natural seat of creative expression, whilst in the second instance, I have to resort to left hemispherical traits to 'construct' the work. Needless to say, I find the latter a most unfulfilling experience, and one that, now I no longer rely upon this sort of work for my main income, I am thankfully able to entirely avoid. This is a good example of the previously discussed issue of when one has to earn a living from one's creative abilities, subjugation of one's true expression may be a price one has, now and again, to pay.

The inspirational nature of music, for me, does not have to be of a specific genre or cultural style to invoke the need to dance: from Haydn to hard rock, or Cossack to Cuban salsa, if it strikes a chord, then I can choreograph to it, even if I have no formal training in those particular dance styles, or have never visited their country of origin. If I were asked to put together some steps without music in the style of, say, Spanish flamenco, I could probably string together some decent moves representative of this genre. However, if you play me a piece of authentic flamenco music, I am likely to come up with a much broader range of steps and moves, with which I may even surprise myself! What is that source for which music is the conduit in this situation? Perhaps this brings us back to the concept of that universal, cross-cultural subconscious that has been said to underlie all fundamental means of communication: if the music was produced by someone whose composition and performance are rooted in this primal phenomenon, and I, as a recipient, am open to the embodiment of its content, then the connection is implicitly made. This brings us back to the issue of whether a performer can remain authentic whilst being versatile enough to take on different styles and genres of music and dance and produce a convincing performance. I posed this question, along with some others, to two musicians with whom I've had several philosophical conversations along these lines and they have both generously agreed to share their thoughts on this subject.

The first is Ben Dawson, a concert pianist and composer who, on the side, has a career playing regularly for film and TV soundtracks; including a brief moment as the soloist in Gershwin's *Rhapsody in Blue* in Baz Luhrmann's film adaptation of *The Great Gatsby*.

As a musician, do you think that authenticity and versatility in performance are mutually exclusive, or is it possible to switch between composers, styles and genres of music whilst remaining true to their essence?

I suppose it depends on how big a canvas you're painting, but I'm of the opinion that musicians broadly fall into two basic categories – those that 'get' music and those that don't. Okay, so you can be a specialist in baroque flute music and you'll understand all the nuances of ornamentation, or you could be an authority on 20th century bagpipe music and would equally understand the minutiae of what makes a good player/ interpreter – but I think, even if you're not a specialist, most educated listeners instinctively know when they're listening to someone who is not necessarily the world's most authentic performer of a certain composer, but a performer who has such ease and skill with the music that you just have to acknowledge the fact that they 'get' it. To that end (from the performer's perspective) if you've had a broad musical education and possess a lively and thoughtful mind you probably want to do a job that will make people notice you as possessing such a mind.

Are there any styles/composers that you feel you would not be authentically able to perform? What is it that you feel or know would make you unable to do this?

Numerous. I just don't tell many people about it. You never let people know where your Achilles heel is do you? I guess the composers I shy away from are those that a) are treated with enormous reverence – Bach and Beethoven leap to mind, for example (although I did get cornered into playing the *Moonlight Sonata* for 2,000 children once) or b) styles that I don't have a particular enthusiasm for as a listener. But then, this is just a personal thing. There are literally thousands of pianists around the world playing Bach and Beethoven in concerts, every day to many, many thousands of people. I'm sure some of these concerts are wonderful, and I'm sure that a certain number are horrific. Either way, I assume that the vast majority of these performers have sufficient self-confidence to go out there and perform these pieces – of which I am deeply envious. Does it mean they perform them authentically (and authentic these days tends to mean historically informed)? I haven't a clue. But then, I'm not one of the purists when it comes to the great and faintly tedious debate of authenticity. Honesty and accuracy, yes. But authenticity? That's a notion that people have waxed lyrically about for 50 years at great length in books and scholarly editions to make themselves feel like they know something you don't.

To answer the second part of your question, I guess it's a matter of self-belief and confidence – which I lack in abundance, despite fleeting on (and off) stage suggestions to the opposite. It's all the art of illusion . . . . Not having grown up playing those composers, not having gone to music college as a pianist and, at the same time, overheard countless hundreds of (mainly young) pianists in my earlier days, talking loftily about them at any opportunity, I feel as though my mind has been put off trying to compete or add to the noise – I'll try my luck elsewhere. For now.

When observing or listening to other musicians, what do you think are the tell-tale signs of an inauthentic performance, other than those related to technical ability?

When I was fresh out of college and full of dubious yet confidently expressed opinions, I used to believe that you could tell the performance you were going to hear by the way the performer walked on to the stage. With students, that tends to remain the case most of the time – they're still working out the art of illusion. However, the older I've got, the more performers I've seen, I've noticed that that theory holds very little water. Personally though, I'm always slightly suspicious of performers that move too much with their instruments or pianists that look toward the ceiling (and stars beyond) and make flamboyant hand gestures. I don't know exactly where it comes from – probably an over-enthusiastic teacher in their formative years who never stopped saying "You must *feeeeeel* the music." Movement *is* essential in performance, for flexibility and muscle relaxation, but is it necessary for expression? To a fairly modest extent, yes – but my cynical side says it's about some people trying to look like they're the real deal – perhaps to convince themselves as well as the audience. Who knows? I've seen some elaborate gymnastics at pianos, and most of it is as hilarious as much as it is distracting. The piano is a mechanical device – I can hit a middle C and let it ring – it will sound the same if I hit it and arch my back and look towards Orion whilst doing air origami with my spare hand. The art of illusion yet again . . .

If you are forced to play repertoire with which you feel little or no connection, how does this make you feel and how does it affect your playing?

I've never been in a situation where I've been forced to play something (as an adult). However, I might take on a concert where I feel indifferent about some of the music in it. There are also times when you're part of a larger group or an orchestra and you actively dislike a certain piece, but you just get over it and get on with it – it's your job. But as a soloist, I've never taken on a piece that I didn't enjoy or like on some level. Even if there's a fairly uninspiring piece that you've been asked to do, and don't want to turn the date down, you can find something to like about it – and if even that fails, just remember you're getting paid to play the piano and you just have to be professional about it: walk out, smile towards the audience, sit down and turn the showbiz button on! Sounds almost mercenary, but that's sometimes how life goes – and I don't mean it in a cynical way. I guarantee you that in a performance, you wouldn't be able to tell the difference from looking at me on stage between a piece I adored and one I loathed. Smoke and mirrors . . .

Do you experience any physiological changes when you feel truly connected to your repertoire? How does this differ from when you are playing repertoire you don't enjoy? Are any physical symptoms exaggerated, either positively or negatively, by the pressures of your personal or work environments?

I've only experienced that almost mystical and fleeting Zen-like state in a performance a few times in my life so far. You never know when it's going to happen, and you certainly can't make it happen. I've been on stage whizzing through the more difficult bits of various concertos with an orchestra playing full-tilt beside me and had the oddest thoughts going through my mind: "What if I play the next bar like an idiot?"; "Is my foot about to slip off the pedal?"; "Did I put enough change in the parking meter?"; "I wonder if my mum is happy with her seat?" I wish I could completely excise these annoying mental distractions whilst playing. I don't know why they're there; they get in the way and serve no purpose, as far as I can tell. But then you realize you're having these thoughts and you tell yourself to shut up and focus – all whilst still playing.

On the exceedingly rare occasions when you do enter that totally relaxed and connected state of being with the music, it's magnificent – and it'll last for a couple of minutes at most (in my experience) and you feel wonderful. You don't think about making mistakes, you just have this almost innate knowledge that they won't happen. Your arms and fingers feel like they're just connected to the piece at a fundamental level, and tension simply doesn't exist. You're in total command and control – the audience doesn't exist. And then it's gone – in a flash. Back to thinking about crap that doesn't need to be in your mind.

Another point worth mentioning is that when you feel truly connected to your repertoire (especially in the learning phase), the more difficult technical things seem to be a little easier to cope with – perhaps because you want to cope with them, or your mind will willingly jump a few more hurdles, both physical and mental, to get you to where you need to be.

What role does improvisation play in your professional life, either in practice or performance? Do you feel liberated by it or does it make you feel out of control? Do you only truly feel 'authentic' when improvising, or do you find this equally achievable playing existing repertoire?

Because I also compose as part of my professional life, it's essential. For me, that's how all music begins – with (informed) improvisation. Sometimes you let the improvisation control you, and sometimes, the other way round. You just have to judge when it's best to do each one. I'm not the sort of person who will record an hour's worth of improvising at the piano and then see what good material I can extract from it. That's the musical equivalent of throwing sufficient shit at the wall and hoping some of it will stick . . . There are some people that do that but it's not my style. The scope for improvisation in existing repertoire is there, it's just a lot smaller. There are so many variables that you can play with without doing the composer a disservice, I think. On a much lesser scale – throwing a curve-ball in performance can be fun if you're with fellow musicians who you know will hear it, react to it and roll with it. It'd be awfully tedious if we plotted and charted out every corner. You have to have a broad idea of what you're going to do, and some corners really do need ruthless working out and precision, but you also have to allow yourself to live in the moment and be spontaneous when you want to be. That's where the joy and life is, and what makes a performance real and unique. I recently played a big romantic concerto and spoke to the audience beforehand and as I turned away from them to sit at the piano and begin, I said (unplanned) to them and the orchestra 'let's see what happens'. I suppose that's how my mind works.

The second contributor is Jon Scott, a drummer who has an established reputation on the UK Jazz scene. He has played for many artists including 2011 MOBO 'Best Jazz' award winners *Kairos 4tet*.

As a musician, do you think that authenticity and versatility in performance are mutually exclusive or is it possible to switch between composers, styles and genres of music whilst remaining true to their essence?

I don't think that authenticity and versatility are necessarily mutually exclusive. There are many situations where they end up being so, but that is more to do with the individual performer prioritizing versatility over a genuine connection with a musical genre: it's easy to fall into pastiche when you don't have a deep understanding of a style, and the solution is usually to simply spend more time absorbing the finer points of that style, broadening your repertoire as both a player and a listener. I think there's something deeper than style which is the key to authenticity – the idea of actually having something to say, and not performing for cynical reasons, but of course in order to express that you need a certain level of comfort in the style in which you're choosing to express it.

Are there any styles/composers that you feel you would not be authentically able to perform? If so, what is it that you feel or know would make you unable to do this?

There are plenty. Generally for the reasons above. Obviously there are always areas with which you have a more natural connection, often through historical exposure or association with certain memories. That simply makes the learning process within that style easier.

When observing or listening to other musicians, what do you think are the tell-tale signs of an inauthentic performance, other than those related to technical ability?

This varies so much with the musician. Some people very much wear their heart on their sleeve when they play, so if you notice them being less visibly connected to the music, that can be a sign. On the other hand, some people compensate for a lack of genuine connection by over-dramatizing the physicality of their performance. I do think it's generally very easy to tell, but the cues which we use to spot this are too subtle to enumerate in this way. You could probably argue that the level of technical ability affects the subtlety of these cues.

If you are forced to play repertoire with which you feel little or no connection, how does this make you feel and how does it affect your playing?

Strangely, if I feel detached emotionally from the music, it's easier to switch into 'practice mode' and keep a conscious eye on the technical aspects of playing, in a way which doesn't happen when the playing situation feels more personal.

Do you experience any physiological changes when you feel truly connected to your repertoire? How does this differ from when you are playing repertoire you don't enjoy? Are any physical symptoms exaggerated, either positively or negatively, by the pressures of your personal or work environments?

This can vary a lot. As above, if I'm not 'feeling it', I can use some spare brain capacity to keep an eye on the physical aspects of the performance. The most noticeable physiological effects are in situations where I'm into the music, but maybe not as experienced as I should be, so I 'try' too hard, and push myself physically in ways which wouldn't happen had I spent more time practicing that particular thing.

Certainly both kinds of pressures affect physical symptoms. Any situation where I'm not psychologically comfortable tends to manifest itself physically in some way, generally for me through shoulder tension. Busy touring schedules can exacerbate this by not allowing good recovery time between gigs, especially when you're carrying drums around day to day, and driving, often on too little sleep.

Do you have a playing 'zone' where conscious thought slips away? How would you describe this feeling and what are the factors that need to be in place for you to get there?

I do, although it's often elusive. The feeling is one of watching yourself play from a distance, or feeling completely connected to the whole of the music rather than just your own part. If I knew what the factors were I'd get there a lot more often :)

What role does improvisation play in your professional life, either in practice or performance? Do you feel liberated by it or does it make you feel out of control? Do you only truly feel 'authentic' when improvising or do you find this equally achievable playing existing repertoire?

As a jazz musician that's the core of what I do. Yes, I feel liberated by it, and yes, I also feel out of control. But those moments of loss of control are the enjoyable ones. It's the idea of trying to get lost and find your way back, while also knowing that some part of you is keeping an eye on what's going on the whole time. This is the area where authenticity is most detectable for me. Playing existing repertoire in an authentic way is arguably less of a challenge than improvising authentically in a particular style. So it's easy to spot a 'stylist' over a genuine improviser. Witness any music college saxophone player who has digested the Charlie Parker *Omnibook* without spending enough time with the recordings of that period.

But no, I don't believe that improvising is the only route to authenticity, it's just maybe one where it can become more apparent.

Both these musicians are echoing many of the concepts we have already discussed, although neither of them had read the content of the book prior to making their contributions. They both relate feelings of physical tension in the moments when they are not completely at one with their repertoire, which is a great example of the PNI system at work. This highlights how musicians who are experiencing symptoms of physical pain need to look beyond just the mechanics of their posture and technique when exploring the causes of their discomfort. Finding a way to connect emotionally with their repertoire may also be a key factor in reducing tension and therefore symptoms.

When creating roles and performing repertoire, it is my belief that those performers who have themselves journeyed through a range of emotional encounters in their lives will actually have a richer depth of experience from which to draw. However, they may also be tapping into some subconscious, universal source of emotional expression embedded within the repertoire that they are performing. In order to maintain harmony in their physiological environment, they will have also needed to explore their own psyche: this will enable them to recognize when they are straying from their own authentic selves. Using this recognition, they will then need to develop strategies for keeping themselves connected with their authenticity and we will explore some examples of these in the next chapter.

For vocalists, there are some interesting issues surrounding the authenticity of the sound they are creating. Singers who perform primarily speech-based material, e.g. jazz, pop and rock, are likely to come from their own habitual ways of expressing, which can be inherently authentic. If they also write their own material, then the sound is likely to be a true reflection of the creator's intention. However, singers who work either in opera or in musical theatre, where they are playing a role, or gig singers who work as 'tribute artists' impersonating the voice of other singers, may be required to create sounds that are further removed either from what their voices do easily or from their own authenticity. In musical theatre, for instance, most shows will have a distinct 'sound' to which the performers all conform. Some singers may have a voice which naturally lends itself well to a particular style and one can often be characterized by others in this way – "She's got a great Cameron MacIntosh sound", etc. When auditioning for shows, performers will often be trying to recreate that 'sound' in the hope of being chosen, but it may not be something to which their voice naturally lends itself. This does not mean that the voice is not a versatile instrument capable of producing many different sounds, but singers should be aware of how much tension is associated with the creation of a particular sound or style for them and take steps to manage this – a good teacher would help them with this. If excessive phonatory effort is required to produce a particular sound, then this may result in vocal strain. The aim should be to sing with 'intention' not 'tension': connecting with the intention of the character should help to allow a tension-free sound. Whether this 'sound' meets the requirements of the production is another matter and finding a compromise is one of the many challenges of being a performer!

In the context of a so-called 'function band', which typically plays covers of existing popular repertoire, the singer may be required to change sound and style between each song. This is a world with which I am very familiar: a typical gig for me could be anywhere from 35 to 50 songs and could contain repertoire from the likes of Ella Fitzgerald and Dinah Washington, through to Dusty Springfield, Amy Winehouse, or Lady GaGa. If it is a solo gig with no male singer, then it may also include male repertoire from artists such as Frank Sinatra, Stevie Wonder and Michael Jackson! I am often also performing songs which have been produced in a recording studio and which have no basis in natural authentic sound and it is these which I personally have always found the most challenging. Retaining authenticity in these circumstances is clearly going to be more of a stretch. I actually quite enjoy the 'character-hopping' that such gigs require, but always run a quick post-performance diagnostic to check for any tension that may have crept in. I will also find time for vocal practice in my own voice to redress the balance. Tribute artists may spend their careers imitating one specific singer, and whilst it may be that they have chosen this path because their voice is a natural fit for the original artist, that is not always the case. I have recently been treating one such performer who chose this path because she bears a strong physical resemblance to the original artist, but vocally, her own sound is quite far removed from that of the singer she is impersonating. This has caused her to suffer from issues of vocal strain as she strives to 'create' a sound which is not a natural fit for her own vocal anatomy. In addition, the voice of the particular recording artist she portrays, (who shall remain nameless), is clearly heavily altered and augmented by the production process, to the extent that it is not actually reproducible live, even by the original artist herself! The voice is an organic instrument and, as such, is very susceptible to stresses and strains. Any contrivance to produce a sound that is far removed from the singer's natural voice and is stretching the bounds of their own anatomy has the potential to produce problems. If one is playing a part in a long-running show or performing a tribute act night after night, using a sound that is being achieved through tension, the results can be damaging over time.

The voice, in my opinion, is one of the most truly expressive parts of who we are. There is a commonly used proverb which says that the 'eyes are the window to the soul', but, for me, the voice tells me so much more about a person than I can glean from their eyes. The eyes can often be well defended – some people have quite a clear 'no entry' sign pinned across them. The voice however, like body language, never lies – even if the words it produces seek to deceive. Many people, particularly in the performance world, contrive a sound for their voice which they feel projects the image of themselves that they wish to convey, but the contrivance in itself is descriptive of the person behind that image. When working with my patients, I find the voice to be most indicative of their current state of mind, and therefore health, even if it is cloaked in a mask: a subtle crack or waver when a particular subject is touched upon; the slightly clenched or choked sound of someone who feels they are not being heard or are lacking control in a situation; the high pattern of breathing and audible breath sounds of someone under stress; the openness and clarity of tone which returns when an issue has been resolved – these are all valuable tools in understanding the subtext of the patient's state of health, regardless of the words being said. The voice is the meeting point of both our emotional subtext and the contrivance of language and is often the arena where the struggle between these sometimes opposing forces is played out. The physiological signs and symptoms produced here are well worth exploring: the next time you have an inexplicably sore throat, perhaps you may correlate this with finding yourself in a situation where you feel you are being subjugated by another and therefore have no 'voice'; or perhaps there is a conversation you need to have with someone which you have been avoiding. Finding or having one's own voice is both a metaphorical and physiological need for health: for those who find themselves removed from this, either by an emotional situation or, in the case of performers, are spending much time recreating the voice of another, it is essential to find the time to return to your own natural vocal expression. I believe that an audience only really truly connects and resonates with a singer when he or she is producing an authentic sound. One may appreciate the vocal dexterity of a performer or marvel at a demonstration of vocal acrobatics, but if it is contrived, then the appreciation will be only on a superficial, rational level. The voices which really touch us, which make us feel like they've reached right inside our body and touched our soul, those are the voices which are authentically driven and may not always be the ones that are deemed to have the most technical prowess. They are simply human and we instinctively recognize them as such. When you allow the voice to be the conduit for the expression of your true self, you may find that any conflicts of language, thought and emotion will be resolved and an inherent connection will be made with those around you.

So what we have seen here is that our body language is inherently authentic when we allow the natural physiological processes of emotional expression and communication their freedom. Our subconscious mind is the initiator of our gestures, our movement (and therefore dance), and music is implicit in their production. Our rational minds can then interfere, via the use of spoken language and 'token' gestures, and this is the point where divisions can occur and 'inauthenticity' can creep in. Whilst the authenticity of the performer remains the keystone in connecting with the audience, many other factors also have to be in place: the composer needs to have created the music out of true emotional expression and any lyrics have to match the message conveyed by the music; the choreographer needs to have channeled the expressivity embedded in the music in the creation of the moves; the playwright needs to have created believable characters and dialogue for the actors to embody; the voice needs to be a true conduit in reflecting the emotions being expressed. When all these things are present, the audience will become awash with the effects of their limbic systems, right hemispheres and mirror neurones, whilst being bathed in a nourishing neurochemical smoothie, and it is then that the performance will become a mutually reciprocal journey.

7

Creating balance and authenticity: the ultimate journey

For a performing artist, creating and retaining balance in the face of all the issues we have explored in this text is really an art form in itself. When working with my patients, I feel the key to achieving this balance is through the creation of harmony and resonance. I use these terms here in the physiological context, but it is no coincidence that these words also pertain to musical terminology. I hope that I have shown, in the previous chapters, that from the vibrant, oscillating nature of our sub-atomic particles, ever in motion, to the spaces between those particles where the potential for resonance is created, to the neurologically driven embodiment of music and gesture which create our ability to communicate via the media of body language and the spoken word, we are, as human beings, not just capable of producing music, we are music. Music is the implicit language of the universe; it provides the context for our emotional expression and it is inherently present in all the tissues of our body. It manifests itself not only in our embodied movements or when playing an instrument and singing, but also in the rhythm of the spoken word and in the very beating of our hearts. When performers are in pain or unwell and this is serving to disengage them from their embodied existence, leaving them with a sense of their body as a series of disconnected parts, then the route back to health is through the regaining of the lost harmony and resonance which will lead to reintegration. By using these concepts, which have a reciprocal context within both our physiology and in music, and with which performers will therefore be inherently familiar, the process of regaining balance becomes less daunting, thereby reducing anxiety and placing performers back in control of their own destiny. Once they realize that they have everything they need to return to full health and when they take the responsibility for this journey, then this may also be the route to a more authentic way of being.

In this chapter, I will not be providing a step-by-step program for achieving balance and authenticity, as this would lead us right back to the left hemisphere-driven, mechanistic approach, which I hope I have shown is not the way to create true artistic expression. Equally, I most certainly do not have all the answers and would not be being authentic by claiming so to do. I just seek to remain open, observe those around me and to share what I see and experience whilst travelling along my own path. What I will do is to suggest some concepts and ideas that may facilitate the reader's own journey to authenticity. A concise, easily digestible guide would deprive you of the joy and satisfaction of your own exploration and would also serve to uphold the myth that mistakes and deviations from the path are somehow negative. Recalling what we discovered in Chapter 5 about the rocky road being the best route to achievement, there are really no mistakes, just lessons to be learned and from which valuable information can be gleaned. Be the creator of your own investigative path and don't outsource your autonomy – remain open to the hidden teachers in life.

For performers experiencing pain or discomfort, the key to recovery is having the awareness and recognition of the true source of these symptoms, remembering that these may not always lie in the obvious. When performers are suffering the pain of an overuse injury, for instance to the muscles, this may only be the most superficial layer of a more complex situation involving their emotional history and their relationship to their craft. As we saw in Chapter 3, pain is a multi-faceted phenomenon and performers must be clear as to all the possible sources of their pain. It may not be enough to reduce the symptoms superficially, via treatment and the adaptation of training behaviors, if the pain is being mediated via more complex issues. If the true source has not been identified and addressed, performers may find themselves in a loop of symptom recurrences which may become increasingly more dramatic as the body shouts to be heard. This process may require asking oneself some difficult questions about one's emotional history and one's true relationship with one's art form, but failure to do so will only lead to a dead end. In Dr Gabor Maté's words:

> We want to be the authoritative person in our own lives: in charge, able to make the authentic decisions that affect us. There is no true responsibility without awareness.[2, p.9]

This awareness should also be directed towards the choices we make in terms of our professional and training environments, the people with whom we choose to surround ourselves and whether those choices are being made by listening to our intuition or by the habits into which we have either fallen or perhaps have been pushed. There should be no blame attached to this investigation, either to ourselves or others, as this serves no purpose but, as Dr Maté says, we must take 'responsibility' for our present position and the choices we make going forwards.

Having respect for one's body is fundamental to this process. Most musicians can take their instruments apart and put them back together again almost blindfolded and lovingly attend to them with regular maintenance and upkeep. There are somewhat fewer musicians who afford this same level of care and understanding to their own bodies and, as I regularly point out to those in my care, whilst replacement parts are easily obtainable for your instrument – one can even buy a whole new one if necessary – replacement bodies are not so readily available, so you'd do well to look after the one you have! Learning something of how your body works and what you can do to look after it is a very worthwhile investment of your time. This doesn't necessarily mean that you have to study in-depth anatomy, but having a basic working knowledge of the body's structure, whilst keeping in mind the context of whole body movement, can open your eyes to the infinite possibilities held within these bundles of buzzing particles which we call home. Appropriate self-care routines can then be developed, such as stretches and exercises, but one is much more likely to undertake such routines if one understands the reasons why they are beneficial. Simply doing exercise routines because you have been told to has the tendency to make them a chore and one which is often soon dropped! When you understand why, then such routines become an autonomously driven exercise, which places you firmly in the driving seat, whilst also giving you the tools to develop and adapt these routines along sound physiological principles. It is also important to ensure that the physical and emotional environments in which we place ourselves are likewise conducive to our health. Whilst it may often be necessary to step outside our comfort zone, if we are aware of this and are therefore able to buffer ourselves from any potentially negative effects, this will serve to safeguard our sense of control and autonomy and minimize the effects on our physiological stress mechanisms. To help us to be discerning in our choices, we also need to recognize the difference between distress, which is potentially destructive and harmful, and eustress, which is usually pleasurable in nature, as these will further help to guide us. Although Hans Selye spent his career studying the diseases caused by stress, he also said:

Stress is not necessarily bad for you; it is also the spice of life.[2, p.xv]

It all comes down to the context of the stress we are experiencing: remember that there is no universal stressor, only our response to it. What terrifies one individual might make another laugh – it is all about our own reaction to it. Such reactions are borne out of our own personal emotional histories, but ultimately these reactions are something over which we have control.

Remembering the valuable concept of space can also be a useful image to have in respect of our bodies. Recalling that, at a sub-atomic level, we contain more space than mass is a powerful way to release the sense of congestion and tension which so often dogs our day to day lives, particularly when experiencing an injury. Removing the focus from the site of pain and turning our attention instead to the potential held within the spaces in the tissues, can help to reduce the anxiety that we have seen is a key part of our physiological response to stress. Pain and injury often lead us to feel that we are out of control and any lack of understanding of the mechanisms involved can exacerbate this sensation. It can also lead to the sense that this is 'happening to us'; that we are somehow under attack from an external source. More often than not, it is our own behavior that has led to our pain, which is often caused by overuse or misuse of a body part. This usually stems from a lack of understanding or lack of awareness of the effect of such behaviors, therefore education is the way to move forwards. Seeking the advice of a professional to help to address the underlying cause of these behaviors is a good first step, but we must also ask some deeper questions of ourselves and our attitude towards our own bodies, as well as our relationship to our craft, in order to find resolution. By doing this, we then can take responsibility for our actions, and therefore our pain, and thus move on from them. However, pain or injury can sometimes be inflicted upon us through no obvious fault of our own, but even in such circumstances we are ultimately in control of our response. Someone may choose to hurt you either emotionally or physically, but how you respond to this is entirely within your control. If you are in the habit of responding dramatically to such situations, then the physiological effects are likely to be equally as dramatic. However, if you choose to respond by removing yourself from the situation and finding some quiet time and space to calm your physiological response, then you render the external stressor impotent and regain the control and autonomy so vital to your health. If in doing this you feel your sense of justice being piqued and find yourself feeling anger and resentment towards your stressor, then there are probably some questions you would do well to ask yourself regarding the boundaries of your defense system. True anger is an important part of our defense mechanism in times of mortal threat, but in reality we are much more likely to be faced with non-mortal threats to which we respond not with true anger, but with anxiety. True anger is displayed and expelled rapidly in the moment, but anxiety is what keeps us 'festering' about an incident long after the immediate threat has disappeared. Animals display anger when defending their territory from a predator, but after the predator has gone, you won't see the animal sitting in the corner muttering to itself about the injustice of the situation, it simply returns to the business of living. 'Self-talk' is a purely human phenomenon and many of us become our own harshest critics. Constantly beating yourself up over your perceived abilities is every bit as stressful as having someone else do it for you – but it's much harder to escape from yourself. Having the awareness to check your responses to both internal and external stressors, and ensuring your reactions are proportional, is essential to reducing unnecessary physiological stress. Finding space within one's own body and also in one's external environment is key to this process. If you are stuck in a situation which is not conducive to your health, then you need to remove yourself from it or find a space to go within yourself where the stress can be neutralized – like the frog, you need to notice that water heating up around you and jump out of the pan!

Rest is the most wonderful healer and is often highly undervalued and misunderstood. The conditioning that most performers undergo during their training often places little or no value on rest and sometimes even bestows it with negative connotations. I myself still wrestle with the gremlins who persistently whisper in my ear every time I try to sit still and relax, telling me that I should be doing something and not just 'lolling' around. Even if I decide to watch a film on TV, I find myself planning all the things I can get done in the next commercial break! I have been conditioned to correlate rest with laziness, which not only devalues it but turns it into a crime in the obsessive, perfectionist world which I have created for myself. Even with all the knowledge I now have of the physiological benefits of rest, I still have to 'talk down' the gremlins before I can really settle, but at least I now get there – eventually! Sleep allows the body to shut down all non-essential activities and get on with the important work of cellular repair and regeneration. Without sleep, the body can only ever paint over the cracks. For our brains, too, sleep is also vital: there is much processing and integration of information that occurs during sleep, as well as the enhancement and consolidation of both sensory and motor memory. Therefore, sleep should not be seen as just a cure for tiredness, it is essential to our physiological wellbeing. However, rest does not necessarily mean lying down and having a good night's sleep or a day-time nap, although both of these clearly have enormous advantages, rest can also be just doing something else – ideally something pleasurable and not attached to any goal. The old adage 'a change is as good as a rest' has much value. If you have spent six hours playing your instrument, why not put it down and go for a walk or call up a friend you haven't spoken to for a while? Remember Hans Selye's warning about the damages of repetitive tasks, both physical and mental – localized rest is essential to avoid wearing out individual parts. He goes as far as to say that no one ever dies of old age, as that, by definition, would mean that all the parts had worn out simultaneously. In reality:

> ... *there is always one part that wears out first and wrecks the whole human machinery*, merely because the other parts cannot function without it.[1, p.432] (author's italics).

If we recall the words of Bill Bryson, who spoke of our atoms as having been around for an exceedingly long time, and how many of our own atoms potentially once belonged to Shakespeare or Beethoven, we see that we never actually die, we just become something else.[5, p.176] A single-celled organism never dies, it just keeps dividing. As humans, we are made up of a huge number of cells and it is actually our complexity that makes us vulnerable. It is only by constantly moving the inevitable stresses of life from one part of the body to another, thereby sharing the load, and by resting either local parts or the whole body in direct proportion to our activities, that we can maximize our health and both the quality and length of our lives. If you find the concept of rest challenging, then you need to ask yourself why that is the case and find a way to resolve any issues that are forming a block to your acceptance of its benefits.

If performers find themselves in the situation where they have lost the joy of performing their craft and it is no longer satisfying their need for expressivity, then they may need to change their relationship to it. Having previously discussed the difficulties of trying to earn a living from something that is your passion, it is in this area that many people, including myself, may choose to make a change. Using my own experience of moving from being a full-time professional performer to a new career path, I have also supported several other performers in making similar journeys. Finding something else that interests you and from which you could make a living (and potentially a much more financially stable one than performing), may free you from the burden of the commercialization of your passion. When you no longer rely upon performing to provide an income, you are free to pick and choose the outlets for your expression. When I chose to move to a career in healthcare, I actually had no expectation that I would continue to perform professionally at all. Whilst I was still loving working as a performer, I could no longer withstand the constant treadmill of endless auditions and the associated anxiety and sometimes desperation over when I would next be in work and for how long. I craved stability and a sense of control over my destiny that performing was not able to give me. However, once I had made the move and the desperation was dispelled, an offer of professional work as a singer with a band landed in my lap. I believe there is much truth in the idea that when you want something to the point of desperation, you somehow block it and it won't happen; but when you change your focus and stop trying, it just comes naturally and unbidden. The job as a singer fitted perfectly around my work as a therapist and dance teacher and enabled me to have an outlet for what I call my inner 'performance monkeys', who were unlikely to remain silent for any period of time. I have continued to sing with bands for the last ten years and absolutely love doing so – it is no longer a job to me (even though I am paid for it), it is pure expression. Whilst other band members are hotly discussing which new jobs are coming up and how to get in on them, I can just sit back and be glad I don't have that worry anymore. What's more, my new profession in healthcare has also become my passion and, in working with performers, keeps me connected to a world in which my roots are firmly embedded. I believe that, following the reciprocal and circular concepts which are threaded throughout this text, even when you make a choice to move in a seemingly opposite direction to where you were, you will inherently return to your natural place, but perhaps just in a different context. If being a performer is your true calling, then you will find it and it will find you, wherever you are and whatever you do. Art is an implicit expression of the human soul and it can be found everywhere if you remain open to it.

A lifelong friend of mine, Francesca Filpi, recently retired after 15 years as a dancer with the Royal Ballet Company. I was in close contact with her throughout this transition and have been working with her on her subsequent projects, which revolve around the opening of a beautiful residential dance centre on the Atlantic coast of Morocco! She very kindly agreed to share her thoughts on making the transition from full-time dancer to teacher and business owner and, despite the fact that she had not read any of the book (which was already completed) prior to answering my questions, she truly echoes so many of the thoughts and concepts raised in the preceding chapters. Here are the questions I posed to her on the subject, along with her responses.

What did you find most difficult about retiring from dance?

I have to confess, dramatic as it may sound, that when I left the company, I literally went through a period of mourning – it was as though a part of me had died, and I no longer knew who I was, or what I was supposed to be. I have always danced, always been a dancer, it was just a fact of my life, like having ten fingers and ten toes! Then suddenly, from one day to the next, I stepped into a great black void, called 'the outside world', where 'normal people' seemed to have a place, but I, myself, felt like a bereft lost soul! Having stepped outside the very protected environment of the 'institution' I had known from being a very young child, I felt a bit as though I were an alien, observing 'normal life' for the very first time. Of course I'd had holidays, and injury times, and a very varied life, with many interests outside my job, but then the world outside was all relative to the fact that I had my identity as a dancer of the Royal Ballet. I was fortunate, in that I have always had a great love for teaching, and had in fact established myself as a teacher alongside my performing career. I always knew that's what I wanted to do eventually and so this helped the transition enormously. But I just wasn't at all prepared for how hard I would find navigating life beyond having my status as a performer, even though, in my mind, I had tried to live this situation a thousand times!

Another big factor was the loss of camaraderie. A ballet company is a very close knit community (in contrast to what the media would have us believe!), and working as a team is fundamental to everyday life, on stage and off. The dressing room is perhaps the biggest stage of all – witness to dramas, excitement, disappointments, nerves (and, of course, sometimes jealousy!) and your fellow dancers are certainly not just colleagues, but they know the ins and outs of (sometimes very private!) areas of your life. It's a bit like an extended boarding school for adults . . . it's probably one of the only professions I can think of where it's possible to start learning together as children as young as three or four, with people that you will end up at full time vocational school with, and then work alongside in a ballet company, until you retire! The ballet world is like a village, and pretty much everyone is known to everyone, either directly or indirectly. Underneath the layers of doubt, uncertainty, and unfairness that every dancer must feel at some stage or other, the overwhelming feeling is that of 'belonging'. Though the daft thing is that sometimes you don't appreciate the extent of this, until you have stepped out of that 'security blanket'. You just know that 'in there' all the people understand and share the same kind of emotions. You don't have to justify yourself or explain things, because they just know! Outside it's a very different scary ball game! All of a sudden, you feel you have to prove yourself all over again, as something else. Just being an ex-dancer is not enough!

Did you feel your personal identity suffered as a result? If so, how did you cope with this issue?

In terms of how I have coped with this 'loss of identity', I am not sure it has been long enough to be able to answer that properly . . . yet!!

What have been the positives about moving on?

Positives about moving on . . . regaining control of my life. As a dancer you are very much a puppet – you are told what to dance, when to dance, how to dance, what to wear . . . there is not much room for making plans outside of the company. When you are young, that is part of the deal that you will-ingly lap up, but your whole life, career, even family and social engagements (and consequently, and most importantly, even your mood!) are in the hands of the director, and there comes a time when you need to be able to take control of your own life. Being a dancer naturally has a tendency to make you rather self-obsessed – you want to look your best, feel your best, do your best. Dancers, through necessity, are prone to self scrutiny and analysis, and every word, every look from the rehearsal director impacts on your performance . . . none of which is good for your self esteem or personal development as a healthy and rounded human being! Obviously I speak from personal experience – there are many dancers out there who are capable of rising above all that . . . but I always felt an over-whelming need to please, and so was very swayed by external feedback. With dancing at a professional level, it´s not quite as simple as handing your homework in on time . . . !

Had you begun to lose the 'joy' of dancing after it being your job for so long?

Since I stopped, I have realized how negative the constant conversation in your head is, and how damaging that can be. Of course our teachers can contribute either positively or negatively to this, but I always felt that the voice inside my own head was my main enemy. I knew that criticism was part of the deal and, again, I almost relished that as part of the 'belonging' and became quite good at building my own little protective bubble around myself. However, I wasn't so good at protecting myself from the voice inside my head. I suppose some people put this to good use, and it is that voice that drives them on, but I found it hindered rather than helped me . . . though whilst I was in the thick of it, I didn't realize to what extent. I often felt like a fraud, because I felt I perhaps wasn't as driven, or as ready to sacrifice so much of my life 'to my art!' as other dancers. It is a career where you feel like a failure if you are not always at the front 'selling yourself' as it were (for want of a better expression?!). You feel you should always be ambitious and desperate to do more, asking for roles, etc. I often felt inadequate and as though I had no right to be a dancer, or have the position I had, because that wasn't how I felt. I just loved dancing and I didn't want to have to be in competition with others, I just wanted to dance for the sheer joy of dancing . . . I felt I never danced my best in solo performances, or certainly never quite enjoyed them in the same way as when dancing alongside others, where you could just give in to the emotion of the moment and *just dance* . . . that, to me, is what dancing is all about. Having to achieve (sometimes impossible for most!) technical feats, rather took that glorious feeling away, and you were left with what seemed like a minefield of potential disastrous steps!

The notion that dance is this wonderful vehicle for personal expression is not always true. There are of course moments of unadulterated joy and roles that make you feel as though you are going to burst with emotion and happiness. But as a professional dancer, you can't pick and choose the roles you dance, and certain roles (or certain costumes!) can, at best, make your day to day life just a case of 'getting through' and, at worst, make you feel as you are though hovering on the brink of insanity, knowing that in so many hours, you will be alone on a huge stage, with all eyes upon you, and you just don't quite know how you are going to live up to expectations.

Now having left the profession, have you developed a new perspective on dance or a new relationship with it?

Before I stopped dancing professionally, I must confess that I couldn't really understand why adults, who were obviously not considering ballet as a career option, would want to go to ballet classes. To me, ballet became something that often made me feel bad about myself: I would stand in the front of the mirror in the morning and the negative running commentary would start in my head. So I just couldn't understand why adults would want to put themselves through that! People used to come and watch performances and would comment how wonderful it must be, to be 'transported' every night. I would often ponder on that as, to us, the shows were not so much a chance to 'be transported' as such, but rather that was our reality – the outcome of months of rehearsal, and more often than not, my mind was one step ahead, systematically working my way through the 'tricky bits', compensating for a broken right shoe, and trying to make sure my left boob didn't pop out of the costume! Of course there were those magical performances where you could completely lose yourself in the music, where everything just seemed to come together, and the complete and utter euphoria you experience is a feeling like none other . . . but it certainly wasn't a nightly occurrence!

It was only when I stopped dancing, that I was fully able to appreciate the capacity dance has to literally 'lift you up to another realm'. In the normal world, I quickly realized what a privilege it was to have my own little vehicle for expression. I would hear beautiful music, and just find myself . . . dancing. No pressure, no expectations, just dancing for the sheer joy of it. It came as quite a shock that there are not many opportunities to be taken out of the everyday humdrum: dance somehow transports you to some higher place, where all the little problems of everyday life recede – it's almost like a form of musical meditation! This led me to start teaching adults, which I find to be the most satisfying and enjoyable teaching I have ever experienced. Adults just want to dance for all the right reasons . . . for the sheer joy of it! And that, to me, is what dancing is all about!

On one of my recent visits back to watch my friends in the company perform, I sat in the audience (which was quite a novelty!) and was completely bowled over by what a different impression you get from out there. It was all so exquisite and moving . . . and professional! I went back to the dressing room in the interval, full of excitement and admiration, only to hear all the girls berating themselves for having messed up that particular step, for having wobbled on that turn . . . I remember feeling so profoundly shocked, that their perception of the performance was so completely different to mine. It wasn't as though I was just a green and novice casual observer: I had, of course, noticed the little things that had gone wrong, but they were so little in the grand scheme of their talent and of the performance as a whole. I actually got quite upset to hear them putting themselves down in such a way and being so hard on themselves, thinking that I had been part of that self critical tirade for so many years, and only now that I had come out the other side, could I see how counterproductive and joy-erasing it all was. I just so wanted them to be able to see the magic that I had just witnessed on stage – the magic that *they* had created. I suppose that is a necessary part of striving for perfection, never being happy with your performance, always thinking you can do better, but it just seems . . . so lopsided!

Do you think there are any issues with the training of young dancers which need to be addressed in order for them to retain the joy of their craft whilst dealing with the pressures of skill acquisition?

In terms of the training of young dancers, I do believe the most important gift a teacher can give a pupil, (aside, of course, from the obvious tools to overcome technical and artistic challenges) is a feeling of self-worth and self belief. So much attention is given to students' physical development and training but, in comparison, very little to the psychological side. And yet, for all the technique training in the world, if your mind isn't properly trained, the body is never going to follow!

There is that old school of thought that putting students down makes them tougher and hungrier to succeed . . . personally that never worked for me: not that the words of any so-called 'mean teachers!' ever really hurt me . . . the voice in my head was far meaner than any of them! So I personally thrived with teachers who encouraged me and made me see that I was capable of doing things, teachers who were on my side, even when perhaps I myself wasn't! Obviously, every student is different and I think it is so important to really understand their character and personality – it is so easy to misinterpret reaction, and make false assumptions as to their feelings. Again it's back to that team work – a pupil and teacher have to make a good team and, together, be excited about creating something beautiful!

Do you have any advice for those pursuing a career in dance?

In terms of advice for those pursuing a career in dance, in particular ballet, it's a sad fact that ballet requires certain aesthetic ideals. I sometimes feel quite angry that the art I love so much can be so cruel and with one technical fell swoop, can strike off scores of wonderfully talented, hard-working and beautiful dancers. I so wish we could go back to the days when dance was all about stirring people's souls and not about having the perfect physique. But the sad fact of the matter is that, unless there is a radical change in perspective, unfortunately, we have to be realistic that that's just the way it is. But within those ideals, don't ever be fooled into thinking that you are not a valid dancer because your legs are not quite long enough; you don´t feel as confident as everyone around you appears; you don't relish certain roles; your turn-out is not perfect. Don't you be the one to question yourself, it's a short career and you don't want to waste a second of it doubting yourself. Grab the opportunity, don't twist yourself in knots by thinking too much and just *dance*. It's the most wonderful thing in the world! This is what I would do differently if I could do it all over again!

This is a wonderfully candid account from someone who has great experience of the life of a professional performer and I am so grateful to Francesca for her honesty in sharing her responses. Hearing her description of the negative self-talk, the overwhelming need to please others and also suffering from the aforementioned 'impostor syndrome', paints a picture which will be very familiar to many performers. Her level of awareness of these issues, though, is one of the many things that make her such a wonderful teacher. Anyone who has ever had the privilege of being taught by Francesca will attest to the vibrant sense of inspiration that she brings to the studio: despite any negative experiences she may have had, she remains a truly authentic ambassador for the joy of creative expression.

For some performers, as for Francesca, becoming a teacher can be a natural step, although others may not be drawn to this path. Being a teacher requires a specific skill set and approach: just because someone is a talented and successful performer does not guarantee that he or she will make a good teacher. Knowing how to do something well is one thing, but being able to convey this to someone else is quite another. Many performers actually use teaching to supplement their performance careers, which puts them in a wonderful position to pass on not just the necessary technical skills, but also the realities of life in the profession. Teaching from experience helps the student not only to have proficient technique, but how to adapt that technique in the face of the environmental challenges they may face in the 'real world'– the so-called 'tricks of the trade'. Others may delay becoming a teacher until they reach the end of their professional performance career, particularly in the dance world where one's career is necessarily shorter. However, it is absolutely vital, especially in the latter case, that one is clear about one's motives for moving into teaching: is it purely because it's the easiest and most obvious thing to do in order to ensure financial security at what can be an otherwise difficult time, or is it because one feels explicitly drawn to becoming a teacher? I have had experience myself in the past of being taught by some individuals who were clearly only teaching because they didn't really know what else to do. Some may have failed to find employment as a professional performer while others may have had their careers cut short due to injury, resulting in their harboring feelings of bitterness and resentment which they then proceeded to 'take out' on their students. These were the classrooms where the 'fear-based' model was very evident, creating an atmosphere of anxiety where I felt scared into achieving rather than being encouraged to succeed for my own sense of accomplishment. When you have set your heart on a career as a professional performer and this has not come to fruition or has come to either a natural or enforced end, it is vital to ensure that you have examined and resolved your own feelings about this fact before you attempt to engage with young students in the early stages of their journeys. Similarly, you must also have considered both the good and bad experiences in your own training and remind yourself of how these affected your own personal development. Simply repeating the behaviors of your teachers may not be the best approach, particularly if they do not hold happy memories for you. It is the responsibility of each generation to improve on the last, and not be tempted to perpetuate old practices in the name of tradition. If your own training caused you anguish and anxiety, you have no right to pass this on to your students. As I mentioned in Chapter 5, all the latest research into talent development shows that a 'fear-based' model is not the way to produce elite professionals – engendering a strong sense of autonomy and control, along with the skills to handle the inevitable pitfalls along the way, is the route to producing healthy performers and to minimizing the destructive effects of perfectionist tendencies and self-abusive behaviors. These young students are the teachers of the future, so we must begin to change the old models, which have no relevance in today's culture, in order to ensure our performers have all the personal and technical skills with which to navigate their careers. Teachers should be mentors to whom their students look up with respect, not fear, and one must be in harmony with the issues of one's own journey before one can become a good mentor.

Crises of identity can often befall a performer who is either retiring from the profession or having an enforced absence due to injury. As previously discussed, many performers do not see their profession as something they 'do', it is who they are. So when the time comes to move on from their professional career, a crisis of identity may follow. We live in a culture that is obsessed with labels – job title, age, income bracket etc. – and people are judged by the criteria they meet rather than who they fundamentally are. As a performer, when you are asked the question "What do you do for a living?" and when your reply is either an actor, dancer, singer, etc., this is often met with 'oohs' and 'ahs' of interest – this is a form of applause which the performer readily soaks up. However, if you feel you are no longer able to legitimately use such a label, then you no longer receive such a reaction and you may find yourself feeling that you lack value. I found myself a victim of this issue when I retired from professional performance and had to check myself every time I was asked the inevitable question, as my default answer had always been "A performer". My new response of "An Osteopath" was not infrequently met with the question "What's that?" – quite different from the applause to which I was accustomed! It just didn't feel like 'me' so I would always qualify it by adding that I had recently retired from being a performer and then the conversation would be back on to what I felt was a more comfortable track. However, now my personal approach is to shun all labels, driven by the fact that I appear to do so many things that it is impossible for me to be defined by just one of them. I use the word 'appear' here as, in reality, I see myself as just one thing – me. My work is divided among many strands, but to me they are all inherently reciprocal and all exist because of one another and are therefore interdependent. On any given day, I could legitimately 'label' myself as an osteopath, university lecturer, speaker, writer, dance teacher, voice teacher, anatomy teacher, performance coach, professional singer, choreographer or author, but none of these really describes who I am. Nowadays, my rather paradoxical and slightly abstruse answer to the question of "What do you do?" is usually "What day is it?"! I enjoy not having a specific label and defiantly resist any attempts to be pigeon-holed, preferring to be free of such categorizations which can often be self-limiting. The only problem I incur with this way of being is when it comes to the ubiquitous form-filling, which plagues our modern lives – there just aren't enough boxes! Having said all this, I still firmly believe that we are all inherently musicians and dancers, by our very nature and in respect of our ancestral roots, and these descriptions are not defined by whether or not you make a living from doing so. If you feel that your very existence is rooted in music or dance, and particularly if you have taken it to the extent of becoming a professional, you will always be a musician or dancer. However, you shouldn't allow these 'labels' to limit you to 'doing' just one thing. You can use your artistic skills in any field of work: in fact, you cannot avoid it. My Osteopathic treatments are based in rhythm and movement, my teaching is performance, my writing is creative expression — art is implicit in everything I do. You can use a label if it's useful for navigating yourself in life, but never let it define or limit who you truly are. Likewise, do not view your artistic skills as being limited to the bounds of a performance arena, but let them infuse all aspects of your life. Labels are just so much decorative icing on a cake, but the cake itself is made up of many different ingredients.

Another issue, which has particular reference to the professional dancer who is at the point of retirement (bearing in mind that for many dancers, this will be at a relatively young age) is one of body image. Leaving aside for the moment the issues of eating disorders and their connection to body image, dancers who are at the peak of their profession and who are perfectly healthy will be accustomed to having a lean physique with good muscle tone as well as a greater than average flexibility and strength. This physique is maintained due to the often rigorous training and performance schedules that are a feature of life as a professional dancer. When one comes to retire, and no longer has a need to engage in daily training, this is likely to have an effect on body shape. Whilst many people may have an image of dancers, and in particular classical ballet dancers, as eating very little, I can assure you that this is not necessarily the case. For a healthy dancer, who is typically working at a high cardiovascular output, a high calorie intake is usually necessary for energy replacement. I personally ate a lot more when I was a dancer than I do now, but as dancers are burning these calories off at a high rate, they don't gain weight. However, when a dancer retires and is no longer burning high amounts of calories, weight gain may occur if alterations are not made to the diet. This weight gain is not necessarily a bad thing and may actually return the dancer to a more 'normal' size, but the look and feel of a changing body shape may be something with which the dancer finds it difficult to come to terms. When one has been so conditioned to 'look' a certain way in order to conform to an aesthetic, this can become rooted in one's identity and when this 'look' is lost, then it can give rise to feelings of shame or even disgust, even in someone who had no obvious issues of body image during his or her career. Dancers are also likely to experience a reduction in muscle tone in the absence of daily training, and this can have the result of destabilizing some of their highly flexible joints which, without the control of the surrounding muscles, can then become painful. They may also begin to notice some stiffening in their joints when flexibility is no longer being trained, which can also lead to discomfort. The compounding effect of all these factors can lead dancers to feeling almost alienated from their own bodies and to a sense that they are falling apart. I have seen many dancers transitioning to retirement in my clinic over the years who find themselves in a situation that, after a relatively injury-free 15 or 20-year dance career, they now feel like all the wheels are coming off, just at the time when they are freed from the bounds of rigorous daily training and want to be enjoying themselves! The key here is to find acceptance of one's new body shape and to realize that any weight gain is representative of your finally being kind to yourself. The drive to be a professional dancer borders on (and often crosses over into) self-punishment, and when this behavior has begun in childhood it is likely to be deeply habituated. A new relationship with your body needs to be reached and learning not to perpetually drive yourself to extremes, whilst ensuring a healthy supply of good nourishment, can actually be a way of thanking your body for all its hard work. Any resulting changes in body shape are an example of this kindness to yourself and should be seen as positive. However, from a standpoint of muscle and joint health, it is also necessary to maintain a certain level of exercise in order to minimize any potential pain and degeneration. The extreme flexibility training, which is a feature of the dance profession, actually serves to destabilize the joints – we exploit the normal stabilizing structures, such as the ligaments, in order to achieve the necessary extreme ranges of movement. However, this lack of stabilization is countered by the targeted muscle strength training that is also a feature of dance pedagogy. When training ceases, muscle tone is lost and this means that the joints are no longer protected. Therefore, the dancer must continue with some targeted joint stabilization exercises in order to keep this protection in place. Just as dancers needed to train up over a long period to achieve the professional level, they also need to 'de-train' at the other end. An abrupt cessation of training can be fraught with difficulties, so a measured de-training program is a wise investment. The cardiovascular system also needs some attention: dancers' bodies are like high-powered sports cars, used to running at high revs. But when they no longer work at such a high output, the system can struggle, sometimes leading to issues of poor circulation. Ensuring that vulnerable areas of the body have adequate muscular support and 'running the engine' (i.e. engaging in some exercise which elevates the heart rate) every once in a while is good practice for the transitioning dancer.

There are many methods and approaches available which can help to support one's journey to achieving health through authenticity and the decision to engage in any one of them will be a matter of personal choice. Yoga, meditation, and spiritual or religious practices etc., may be useful in facilitating a journey towards a better relationship with the self, but we must be clear about our motives for such choices. Many such practices have been hijacked by the modern Western world as a shortcut to achievement, which is superficial at best. Iain McGilchrist speaks of modern religion as having begun to attribute material answers to spiritual problems and also of the movement of religious practices towards utility, i.e., how they can support our acquisitional behavior. He continues:

> Thus, 15 minutes Zen meditation a day may make you a more effective money broker, or improve your blood pressure, or lower your cholesterol.[9, p.441]

If we lose the implicit metaphorical nature of such spiritual practices, we are at risk of remaining stuck in our current behaviors and not moving beyond to a more embodied relationship with ourselves. If we simply use these practices just so we can tell ourselves that we are 'doing something positive' towards improving our state of mind, and therefore health, we may also be using them to ignore or distract us from the negative. You may recall from Chapter 3 that it is only by addressing the negatives that we can hope to truly understand ourselves.

The analytical psychologist, Carl Jung (1875–1961), is known to have said of this same subject:

> People will do anything, no matter how absurd, in order to avoid facing their own souls. They will practice Indian yoga and all its exercises, observe a strict regimen of diet, learn the literature of the whole world – all because they cannot get on with themselves and have not the slightest faith that anything useful could ever come out of their own souls. Thus the soul has gradually been turned into a Nazareth from which nothing good can come.

Merely having a good diet, reading self-help books and filling your diary with yoga, Pilates and meditation classes will only be of limited benefit unless you take the time to explore your own emotional history. The above practices are about the future and can certainly be of benefit in moving forwards if approached in the right way, but it is to your past that you must look to answer some of the deep, and potentially very difficult, questions about the events and experiences which have helped to create the person you are today. Without resolving these, your body will continue to create the same, habituated physiological responses that can erode your potential for true health and harmony, no matter how many supportive practices you choose to undertake.

What I hope I have shown throughout this book is that our biology is derived from, and is intimately woven into the world around us, and that artistic expression is an implicit part of who we are. Expression through music and movement forms the basis of our interaction with others and with nature itself and we are in a constant cellular dialogue with everything around us. When we are truly engaged with art, what we are really experiencing is love. Love is about connection, either in viewing something of beauty or in a reciprocal nature with another being, and it is an essential element for health – without it, we wither. So when we begin to reduce art to a 'concept' rather than a 'metaphor' and thus turn it into a commodity, then this is a rejection of love and will ultimately lead to disharmony and ill health, not just as individuals but as a society. So if artistic expression is a fundamental part of ourselves as individuals and serves as a universal language to create social bonds both locally and cross-culturally, then it is also the ultimate route to authenticity for us all. Territory and wealth, on which so many wars are predicated, do not produce health and happiness, they simply enclose and limit us and engender defensive behaviors that will ultimately be reflected in our biology. If one is truly in balance and harmony with oneself and one's surrounding environment, then there is no need to struggle for control and power. Authentic art is at the root of all human expression and it is only when we return to an open dialogue with it, and cease to connect it with targets and goals, that we can experience a return to harmony, both personally and globally.

Over the last seven chapters, we have explored a range of concepts from the fundamentals of human social communication to our biological development, how these concepts affects the way we interact with the world around us and how all of this relates to our health and wellbeing. I hope I have shown that the route to authenticity is in the exploration of our personal histories and that authenticity itself is fundamental to our health and longevity. I hope also that I have shown how art is implicitly embedded in all that we are and, when we are in harmony with art, how it can also serve as the conduit to regaining the connection to our authentic selves. Ultimately, I hope that in reading this book you will have gained some new insights that may be the spark for further lines of enquiry that will help you to begin or to continue your own journey. I will leave you with some thoughts that have been of help to me and may be of help to you in what I hope will be an interesting voyage of discovery.

Retain a fascination for the unexplained marvels of the human body, such as we had as young children before self-consciousness and acquired knowledge had begun their erosive course and anything was possible. This will help to ensure that we remain open to the vast potential that is held within and not limit our capacity to grow and heal.

View pain and injury as an opportunity to heal. These are just questions posed by the body and, in seeking the answers, you may find great rewards. They can teach you acceptance and responsibility and lead you to new heights of physical and emotional awareness. Don't out-source your health – accept what medicine has to offer, but only as an additional support to your own responsibilities.

Resist the tendency to become limited by the labels that society at large, or those in your personal environment, see fit to place upon your shoulders. This will help to protect your sense of self, and therefore autonomy, by freeing you from the bonds of expectation.

Ensure that any anxiety you feel is both relevant and proportional. Anxiety is a vital tool for our survival, but we all too often experience it unnecessarily. Reawaken the connection with your intuitive self, listen to the messages of the body and chose a proportionate response. Don't make unnecessary withdrawals from your Adaptation Energy account.

Find outlets for your creativity that have no agenda other than the pure joy of expression. This will engender harmony and resonance within your own body and therefore in your interactions with others. Joy is contagious, so let that be the gift that you share with those around you.

Take a journey to the roots of your authentic self, accept what you may find there and then telegraph this authenticity through the very resonance of your body. This will ultimately lead you back to the beginning of this circular journey, back to the very essence of who you are.

Once you have the sureness of who you are, then this will be all that you need – it is the only thing on which we can rely and it is infinitely more powerful than fame or material wealth.

I believe that authenticity has a greater healing power than any medicine and will bring you an implicit harmony and resonance which will spread to all those with whom you come in contact. When channeled into artistic expression, this authenticity will reciprocally connect you with any audience by physiologically drawing them into the process. Then, between you, you will create the most powerful performance on earth.

References

1. Selye, H. (1978) *The Stress of Life* 2nd Edn. New York: McGraw-Hill, p. 320. ISBN: 0-07-056212-1.

2. Maté, G. (2003) *When the Body Says No: Exploring the Stress-Disease Connection.* Hoboken, NJ: John Wiley. p. 6. ISBN-13: 978-0-470-92335-1.

3. Marchant, J. (2013) The pursuit of happiness. *Nature.* 503: 468–460.

4. Bowlby, J. (1988) *A Secure Base: Clinical Applications of Attachment Theory.* London: Routledge. p. 68. ISBN: 0-415-00640-6.

5. Bryson, B. (2004) *A Short History of Nearly Everything.* London: Black Swan Books. p. 176. ISBN: 0-552-99704-8.

6. Cropper, W. (2001) *Great Physicists: The Life and Times of Leading Physicists from Galileo to Hawking.* Oxford: Oxford University Press. p. 245. ISBN-13: 978-0195173246.

7. Tolle, E. (2011) *The Power of Now: A Guide to Spiritual Enlightenment.* London: Hodder & Stoughton. p. 113. ISBN-13: 978-0340735509.

8. Arnold, M. (1852) Self Dependence. Lines 31–2.

9. McGilchrist, I. (2010) *The Master And His Emissary: The Divided Brain And The Making Of The Western World.* New Haven, CT: Yale University Press. ISBN-13 978-0300168921 (pbk).

10. Kinsbourne, M. (1988). *Cerebral Hemisphere Function.* Cambridge: Cambridge University Press. ISBN-13: 978-0521364157.

11. Schlaug, G., Jancke, L., Huang, Y., et al. (1995). Increased Corpus Callosum Size in Musicians. *Neurophysiologia* 33(8): 1047–55.

12. McManus, C. (April 14, 2012). Is it True that Left-handed People are Smarter than Right-handed People? *Scientific American.* [Retrieved: September 2013].

13. Hecht D. (2010) Depression and the Hyperactive Right-Hemisphere. *Neurosci Res.* 68(2):77–87. doi: 10.1016/j.neures.2010.06.013. Epub 2010, Jul 21.

14. Clifford Rose, F. (2010) *Neurology of Music.* London: Imperial College Press. ISBN-13: 978-1848162686.

15. Nietzsche (1996) *New Nietzsche Studies*. New York, NY: Fordham University. pp. 129–30. http://faculty.fordham.edu/babich/nns_journal_description-2011.html [Acessed March 2015].

16. Cowper, W. 1731–1800.

17. Einstein, A. (1949) *The World as I see it*. pp. 1–5.

18. Buck, P. (2001) quoted in: Karl Inglesias *The 101 Habits of Highly Successful Screenwriters: Insiders Secrets from Hollywood's Top Writers*, p. 4.

19. Feist, G.J. (1999). The influence of personality on artistic and scientific creativity. In R.J. Sternberg (Ed.), *Handbook of Creativity* 3rd Edn. Cambridge: Cambridge University Press.

20. Burton, R. (1883) *The Anatomy Of Melancholy*. Philadelphia, PA: E. Claxton & Co.

21. Roiphe, K. (2012) The Seven Myths Of Helicopter Parenting. *Slate*. http://www.slate.com/articles/double_x/roiphe/2012/07/madeline_levine_s_teach_your_children_well_we_are_all_helicopter_parents.html [Accessed March 2015].

22. Levine, M. (2012) *Teach Your Children Well: Parenting for Authentic Success*. New York, NY: Harper Collins Publishing. ISBN-13: 978-0061824746.

23. Clance, P.R. & Imes, S.A. (1978). The impostor phenomenon in high achieving women: Dynamics and therapeutic intervention. *Psychotherapy: Theory, Research and Practice*. 15(3): 241–7.

24. Gladwell, M. (2008) *Outliers*. New York: Little Brown & Company. ISBN-13 978-0316017923.

25. Ericsson, K.A., Krampe R.T. & Tesch-Römer, C. (1993). The Role of Deliberate Practice in the Acquisition of Expert Performance. *Psychological Review* 100(3): 363–406.

26. Chase, W.G., & Simon, H.A. (1973). Perception in chess. *Cognitive Psychology* 4: 55-81.

27. Stoeber, J., & Eismann, U. (2007). Perfectionism in young musicians: Relations with motivation, effort, achievement, and distress. *Personality and Individual Differences* 43(8): 2182–92.

28. Flett, G., Hewitt, P., Oliver, J., & Macdonald, S. (2002). Perfectionism in children and their parents: A developmental analysis. In G. Flett & P. Flett (Eds.), *Perfectionism: Theory, Research, and Treatment*. Washington, DC: American Psychological Association. pp. 89–132.

29. Song, K. (2004). Study Finds Perfectionists at Higher Risk for an Array of Problems. *The Seattle Times*. May 12, 2004. http://community.seattletimes.nwsource. com/archive/?date=20040512&slug=healthperfectionism12 [Accessed March 2015].

30. Marcus, M. Loucks, T.L. Berga, S.L. (2001) Psychological correlates of functional hypothalamic amenorrhea. *Fertility and Sterility* 76(2): 315. http://www.science-direct.com/science/article/pii/S0015028201019215 [Accessed March 2015].

31. Collins, D. & MacNamara, A. (2012) The Rocky Road to the Top: Why Talent Needs Trauma. *Sports Medicine* 42(11): 907–14.

32. Newman, J.H. (1851) *Lectures on the Present Position of Catholics in England*.

33. Heidegger, M. 1889–1976.

34. Darwin, C. (1872) *The Expression of the Emotions in Man and Animals*. London: Murray.

35. Bruner, J. & Tagiuri, R. (1954) The Perception of People. In G. Lindzey (Ed.), *Handbook of Social Psychology*. Cambridge, MA: Addison Wesley.

36. Ekman, P., Richard Sorenson, R. and Friesen, W.V. (1969) Pan-Cultural Elements In Facial Displays Of Emotion. *Science* 164(3875): 86–8.

37. Napier, J. (1980). *Hands*. Princeton, NJ: Princeton University Press. p. 166. ISBN-13: 978-0691025476.

38. Libet, B. (1985) Unconscious cerebral initiative and the role of conscious will in voluntary action. *The Behavioral and Brain Sciences* 8:529– 536. http://self-pace.uconn.edu/class/ccs/Libet1985UcsCerebralInitiative.pdf [Accessed March 2015].

39. McNeill, D. (1992) *Hand and Mind: What Gestures Reveal about Thought*. Chicago, IL: University of Chicago Press. p. 245. ISBN-13: 978-0226561325.

40. Fast, J. (1971) *Body Language*. London: Pan. p. 92. ISBN: 0-330-02826-6.

41. Streisand, B. (1973) *The Way We Were*. Documentary. DVD.

42. Lakoff, G. & Johnson. M. (1999) *Philosophy in the Flesh: The Embodied Mind and Its Challenge to Western Thought*. New York, NY: Basic Books. p. 6. ISBN: 0-465-05674-1 (pbk).

43. Graham, M. 1894–1991.

About the author

Jennie Morton
BSc (Hons) Osteopathy, UCL Honorary Lecturer MSc Performing Arts Medicine (Division of Surgery and Interventional Science)

Jennie Morton began her career as a Ballet dancer before moving into musical theatre and still works as a professional singer. She is now an Osteopath specialising in the treatment of performing artists as well as coaching performers from student to elite level. She uses her detailed anatomical knowledge to optimise performance and reduce injury risk.

She is an Honorary Lecturer for the MSc in Performing Arts Medicine at UCL, Chair of the Membership Committee for the Performing Arts Medicine Association (PAMA), sits on the Education and Training Advisory Group for the British Association for Performing Arts Medicine (BAPAM) and the Health and Wellness Committee for the International Society for Music Education (ISME). She is the founder of www.healthyperformers.com.

CPSIA information can be obtained
at www.ICGtesting.com
Printed in the USA
FSOW02n1158040118
43057FS

9 781909 082472